Advance Praise

"In *Turn Up for Freedom*, E Morales-Wil[...] roadmap to healing, wholeness, and lea[...] and femmes and those who love and provide guidance for them. Some parts memoir, other parts anecdote and political toolkit—but all parts love—this book leaves its readers with the confidence and the preparation to both understand and take on a world that is designed to render them defenseless. It is a gift." —**Tarana Burke**, founder and Chief Vision Officer of me too. International and author of *Unbound: My Story of Liberation and the Birth of the Me Too Movement*

"At the heart of *Turn Up for Freedom* is the power of Black and Brown working-class girls—cis and trans—to organize for individual and collective freedom. E Morales-Williams writes, 'their injustices are the least understood,' underscoring structural violence, racism, patriarchy, and transphobia. Grounded in the organizing experiences of TUFF Girls, an intergenerational group in North Philadelphia, the book presents principles and tools that guide the work of awakening collective power. Black and Brown girls emerge as powerful and central participants in the movement for social justice. *Turn Up for Freedom* is empowering, insightful, and necessary." —**Iris Morales**, activist and community organizer, educator, and author of *Revisiting Herstories: The Young Lords Party*

"Amid US educational policy assaults seeking to blacklist global histories of liberation struggles across race, sexuality, and gender, E Morales-Williams delivers insurgent wisdom borne from years of inspired collective study and practice with the youth they served. An intimate testimony, insightful syllabi, and interactive guidebook centering Black girls and gender-expansive youth, *Turn Up for Freedom* is the revitalizing platform to carry its primary audience over the threshold between understanding the unfair and unfinished world they inherit and incubating a renewed vocabulary of resistance necessary to incite mass revolution in their lifetimes. A magnificent and most-needed blueprint for intersectional, healing-centered, joy-filled youth organizing." —**Christopher R. Rogers**, PhD, National Steering Committee, Black Lives Matter at School and coeditor of *How We Stay Free: Notes on a Black Uprising*

"E Morales-Williams' consistent commitment to support young people by imagining and practicing their freedom dreams through healing justice work is a tremendous gift to all abolitionists fighting systems that destroy our humanity, from the constant attacks on Black girls' identities and existences. *Turn Up for Freedom* shines a light on the journey to fight for our liberation—from the womb to the playground, the classroom, and all of the spaces that are battlegrounds for survival, to Say Our Names, and protect our autonomy!

E has dedicated years in holding space in fellowship as part of the collective work and struggle to transform our communities—first by transforming ourselves with each other. E sheds light on the courage, lessons and experiences, and beautiful legacies of Black queer folks doing the work to center, organize, and defend Black girls overlooked by our society. *Turn Up for Freedom* makes beautiful investments in Black cis, trans, and queer girls, femmes, and nonbinary communities so they may see themselves in the future, protected, defended, healed, and ready to stand in their beauty and dignity, unapologetically. This book is a gift to the hearts and minds of young people in Philadelphia and everywhere! *Ashe!*" —**Saudia Durrant**, senior campaign strategist at the Advancement Project

"What a powerful demonstration of Morales-Williams' commitment to Black and Brown girls, femmes, and gender-expansive youth. Tracing the evolution of TUFF Girls creates a platform for deep political learning and persistent activism while simultaneously showing the path to humanism through compassion and love. This is a testament to all that we are now and will become in our connection as beings who strive for liberation and joy—for all." —**Clarice Bailey**, PhD, cofounder, *Girls Justice League*

TURN UP FOR FREEDOM

TURN UP FOR FREEDOM

Notes for All the Tough Girls*
Awakening Their Collective Power

E Morales-Williams

Brooklyn, NY
Philadelphia, PA
commonnotions.org

ISBN: 978-1-942173-83-0 | eBook ISBN: 978-1-942173-99-1
Library of Congress Number: 2023941769
10 9 8 7 6 5 4 3 2 1

Common Notions
c/o Interference Archive
314 7th St.
Brooklyn, NY 11215

Common Notions
c/o Making Worlds Bookstore
210 S. 45th St.
Philadelphia, PA 19104

www.commonnotions.org
info@commonnotions.org

Discounted bulk quantities of our books are available for organizing, educational, or fundraising purposes. Please contact Common Notions at the address above for more information.

Cover design by Josh MacPhee
Layout design and typesetting by Suba Murugan
Printed by union labor in Canada on acid-free paper

Look at what they did to my sisters
Last century, last week
They love how it repeats
Look at what they did to my sisters
Last century, last week
They make her hate her own skin
Treat her like a sin
Oh ah

But what they don't understand, what they don't
understand
But what they don't understand, what they don't
understand
But what they don't understand, what they don't
understand
See what they don't understand
See she's telepathic
Call it Black girl magic
Yea she scares the gov'ment
Deja Vu of Tubman

—Jamila Woods, *Black Girl Magic*

It is our duty to fight for our freedom.
It is our duty to win.
We must love and support one another.
We have nothing to lose but our chains.

—Assata Shakur, *Assata: An Autobiography*

For my family: my grandmother, Dorothy Gibson; my great grandmother, Concepcion Algarin; and my sister, Tracy James.

For all my comrades helping children make sense of their purpose and power while dismantling empire.

And for all the tough girls of North Philly and around the world.

CONTENTS

Dear Reader,

I initially started to write this book for the youth leaders who were involved with an intergenerational collective I started in 2014. It was called TUFF Girls, and TUFF stood for Turn Up for Freedom. If there is any part of you that got excited or even curious about that name, then this book is for you. The title of this book has an asterisk to spark curiosity about girls* and hopefully bring you here. Here is where I share how I'm defining girls*: I mean all girls who look inside their heart and see themselves as such. Whether you were assigned female at birth (AFAB) by a doctor or not, this book is for all the tough girls awakening to their collective **power**. Period.

At the start of TUFF Girls, the Black Lives Matter **movement** was taking to the streets around the country. It was waking up the desire in young and old people to defend Black lives from police and state violence. Social **movements** like this occur when huge amounts of people are willing to work together to create change, such as the rebellions on plantations led by enslaved people or the Black Power **movement** of the 1960s. **Movements** are the only way we have seen some of the big shifts in our culture and society. As lawmakers attack **trans** youth with legislation and ban books from the Black radical tradition in schools, it's clear we still have a long way to go.

Our vision for TUFF Girls was for them to be a part of the **movement** work here in Philly. We had five **principles** in TUFF Girls to help us all do this self and collective work. However, I felt like the way I was talking about it during our time together either wasn't clear or was overwhelming. It was one thing to understand the **principles**, but what did it mean to practice them when you are feeling insecure or angry or hungry? How about when the community around you is still struggling? Even I struggled with that.

I had hoped a collaborative book project could help ground our conversations about emotional and political freedom. As we sunset and close out TUFF Girls, this text becomes a history book of us and other collectives experimenting with freedom work, as well as a guidebook as you look at your own inner and outer reality. Hopefully, reading about some experiences of your peers organizing unlocks something new in your imagination. For your generation and the next.

For some folks who came up in the Black Lives Matter **movement**, they have felt betrayed since they still don't see change after so much organizing and protesting. Some have felt used or overworked in their organizations or they have seen more conflict than unity from their comrades. As powerful as it felt to be in TUFF Girls, it was also hard for these same reasons. Every **movement** has experienced this, but with the right reflection, we can learn so much about how we can struggle better and struggle well together.

So, this book is my reflection and thank you to TUFF Girls for their open hearts, their work, and their honesty; the collective taught me how to be more intentional and accountable. This book is also my apology for the pressure I put on them to join **movement** work when they were not always ready or when they did not feel seen. It is my invitation to them—and to you—to experiment with **movement** work that inspires you and connects you to your purpose, **power**, and community. Last but not least, it is a reminder to myself, and perhaps you, that to turn up for freedom is indeed tough, at times messy, and so worthwhile.

Towards healing and resistance,

E Morales-Williams, aka Dr. E

PREFACE

I started TUFF Girls for several reasons, all of which are tied to my deep love for Black and Brown girls and **gender-expansive** youth.[1] The world has a deep and particular fear of them, which makes this love also particular. As a Black girl who transitioned into a **nonbinary** person in adulthood, I also know and have experienced the ebbs and flow of this fear.

But I had a chance to really **study** it as I did research in graduate school. I did a **study** on the community center that raised me as a child of the Bronx, NY. Since it was such an important place for me to have fun and discover my strengths and talents as a youth participant, and later as a youth worker, I was hoping to gather information or data to write a positive story about community centers. I wanted to prove that community centers were important places for girls of color, especially those living in places like the Bronx.

Instead, I found youth workers who judged the girls as loud, ratchet, or too "fast and grown." I saw boys harassing girls—verbally and physically; rating their bodies, as well as the bodies of youth workers; and to top it off, the male counselors laughed it all off. Because the counselors were less concerned with holding boys accountable, they enjoyed a closer relationship with them. Kids and counselors shouted

---

[1] Gender-expansive youth refers to young folks who identify outside of the gender binary of girl and boy. It includes youth who identify as trans, nonbinary, genderfluid, genderqueer, two-spirit, etc.

homophobic and transphobic comments as jokes or as threats without any consequences. As a researcher who had also grown up there, I wondered if the community center had always been like this, and if I was just noticing it because I no longer valued a "boys will be boys" mindset and felt less shame about being queer. While I couldn't write the story I had hoped, I did arrive at an important discovery.

Black and Brown **cis girls** were eager for safe spaces where they felt good in their bodies and could share their lives and stories without judgment. While none of the youth there identified as **nonbinary** or **trans**, it was clear there were even fewer safe spaces for them. In the study, I concluded that all of these youth and the adults in their lives could be a better support system to each other if they better understood where our politics or beliefs about gender and **sexuality** come from, and how **trauma** impacts us differently. I knew someday I wanted to help create that space, I just didn't know how.

During the last year of writing the book about my hometown community center,[2] I became the education director of a community center in North Philadelphia that focuses on youth, kindergarteners through eighth graders. It was a dream job since I felt like I was back home. North Philly and the Bronx have a lot of similar economic and social struggles *and* cultural legacies of Black and Brown resilience. Like a lot of struggling buildings in our communities, it was a difficult job since it didn't have a lot of structure

---

[2] The book I am referring to here was my PhD dissertation, "Tough Love: Young Urban Women of Color as Public Pedagogues and their Lessons on Race, Gender, and Sexuality" (2014). A dissertation is a kind of research book you write in graduate school to earn a PhD and show your expertise and new knowledge about a topic.

or organization. We needed more staff, and my white boss did not have his heart invested in the work the way that I did. This made making certain changes more difficult since he was not able to understand the vision I had for the space. As a white man who had not attempted to build relationships with parents or the community that the center served, he joined a longer history of white leadership that wants to "help" Black and Brown people from their own comfortable positions and their own moral superiority. It felt like my soul was suffocating and out of respect for myself, I decided to leave my position at the end of the year. When June finally came, there was relief, but there was also a deep sadness. The children asked why I was leaving. I was honest with the middle school girls,[3] because I felt they could understand leaving a position where someone wanted to keep you small. They did, somewhat, but they were still disappointed. As was I.

I channeled those feelings into a written proposal to start a club at the community center. This would allow for a lot more freedom in bringing my learnings from that initial **study** into reality. Plus, I would still be able to work with the North Philly community I had come to love, albeit a very specific age group: middle and high school kids.

Middle school felt like an important priority because when it comes to working with youth, they are the least chosen. In fact, they are usually avoided. Even middle school students say they wouldn't want

---

[3] These were all cis girls. Much like the summer camp I studied for my dissertation work, none of the youth identified as nonbinary or trans, likely because they did not feel safe to do so or may not have come to that level of awareness just yet. For example, I did not become connected to and aware of being nonbinary until adulthood.

to teach middle school. Most doctors, psychologists, teachers, and parents will tell you it's a tough age. Many say it's because of all the physical and emotional changes which are uniquely different to each person. This is why it would also be the perfect age group for TUFF Girls to focus its energies on. The model for TUFF Girls was based on the lessons learned from my years working out of community centers, my early work in **movement** building for Black liberation, as well as other radical youth spaces like SOLHOT (Save Our Lives, Hear Our Truths), A Long Walk Home, Girls for Gender Equity, Girls Justice League, Youth United for Change, Philadelphia Student Union, and many others.

We held this space for five years, and in 2020, after serious reflection and hard conversation, we started an intentional closing of our program. We called this process our "sunsetting." We spoke with every alumnus about this choice, paid them for their time as they also reflected, and then allowed them to take our remaining funds and decide what happened to them. Through a collective process they decided to give a large portion of funds to the Girls Justice League and invest in their own education. Most importantly, alumni along with other youth from Philadelphia and New York read this book, offered edits, questions, suggestions, and their voices. Our collective hope is that this book is not only a part of our sunsetting process, but our living legacy, an offering to the **movement** of Black futures and all the tough girls who are trying to get free.

INTRODUCTION

Being my full and authentic self feels like freedom.
—Zaya Wade

If it feels right in your body, take a deep breath with me. I'm going to keep inviting you to do that throughout this book. Breath is medicine. It brings you back to your body. It slows a racing heart. It clears a foggy mind. It helps you remember who you are. It helps you remember your **power**. Every time we remember the breath, the medicine, we grow:

peace
clarity
healing
freedom inside ourselves.

This is a book that most youth and adults can read and say, "I feel that." That is because this is a book inviting you to heal and to organize for your dignity and to be respected, something so many of us are craving. It's full of stories, poems, hard facts, gentle reminders, and most importantly, tools. Anyone can use these to nourish themselves and others as injustices happen on a daily basis.

Yet, often it is you, Black and Brown girls—cis and trans—whose injustices are the least understood by the world. So, I welcome everyone who has come and who has a desire to get free, but I'm calling all my Black and Brown girls to the front of the room. I see you and I feel you. I wrote this to you as a former

Black girl who taught in high schools and community centers in the hood. And I wrote this book—with the help of the community—especially for my tough girls in the hood because there are not enough spaces that allow you to process the uniqueness of your pain. The goal here is to help you transform it towards emotional and political freedom.

Before Europeans colonized the continent of Africa, many societies did not have a strict gender system of "girl and boy."[1] This belief is called the **gender binary**.[2] Countries like Ghana, Nigeria, Burkina Faso, and Ivory Coast have historically understood that gender could exist on a spectrum like the colors of a rainbow. Your gender did not have to match with your sexual organs. According to Shaman Malidoma Somé from Ghana, gender is "purely energetic . . . one who is physically male can vibrate female energy and vice versa."[3] Part of the violence of **colonization** and slavery was that it took away our right to determine how we owned our bodies and even how we understood our gender. Gender is a journey and I hope you give yourself permission to walk it with curiosity and care. The impact of this colonized violence is exactly why this book is written specifically for all the girls. This too is a part of the emotional and political freedom I'm talking about.

---

[1] Oyèrónké Oyěwùmí, *The Invention of Women: Making an African Sense of Western Gender Discourses* (Minneapolis: University of Minnesota Press, 1997).

[2] Alok Vaid-Menon, *Beyond the Gender Binary* (New York: Penguin Workshop, 2020).

[3] Shanna Collins, "The Splendor of Gender Non-Conformity in Africa," *Medium*, October 10, 2017, https://medium.com/@janelane_62637/ the-splendor-of-gender-non-conformity-in-africa-f894ff5706e1.

Each chapter carries lessons learned from gathering Black and Brown girls[4] front and center, trying to figure out how we continue a legacy of facing injustice head on and creating soulful connections in the face of so much grief. I, we, don't have all the answers. What we do have are the stories of people who dared to refuse a society where we are quiet and tolerant about the **harms** of poverty, **racism**, and **sexism**.

Let me start with my story so that you know why I was gathering tough girls in the first place.

I am a Black unicorn. I'm from a Puerto Rican mama bear who named me Erin.
I named myself Mari when I was 18, though. Renamed myself E at 36. I am from my momma's fire.
The one East Harlem started in her.
The one she tended to as she stretched our life across the 3rd Avenue Bridge, into the Bronx,
into the territory of the Italian mob and the fighting Irish,
a land where the Lenape natives once lived, before they were conquered by European greed.

I am from my father's calming presence, the one he breathed into his Black body
as he learned to swim north in cold waters.
All the way from the southside and always in the southside.
South Miami, South Philly, South Bronx. Until he too left the city away from our people.
I am from the friendship my parents had because they made the choice to not marry.
I am from their strength, but like them and like you, I am from a broken world.

I am from stolen Africans forced onto stolen land.
I am the dreams and nightmares of all of my **ancestors**.

---

[4] Inside of TUFF Girls, these were cis girls. In my time as a high school teacher, this included cis and trans girls.

Like many of them, I am a survivor of wars I did not
    start, on land that is not mine.
I am a small drop of history, telling a story of freedom
    work in a country that has made so much of the
    world unfree.
I'm Harriet's daughter. And Lolita's. And Sylvia's. And
    Ella's. And Malcolm's.

I'm from the quirky teenager who went to racist private
    schools and dirty public schools.
I'm from all the times I looked in the mirror and
    wished my perm could make my roots lie more flat.
The icky feeling of older men trying to catch a feel in a
    packed train car racing downtown.
The rush that comes from watching my peers brawl
    with each other in the hallway between classes.
Over boys. Over a rumor. Over a look.
I'm from Friday night dance classes at Kips Bay Boys
    & Girls Club.
Second place winner of Jimmy's Bronx Cafe Booty
    Shaking Contest: Teen Night Edition.
I am a memory of NYC in the nineties. Bazooka
    bubblegum and blood-stained concrete, all mixed
    together.

I am from the new questions I started to ask myself as
    I got older.
Like, why do grown men create booty shaking contests
    for teen girls?
Like, what *does* freedom really mean—for all Black girls?
I'm from the courage it took to leave home and ask
    those questions, over and over and over again,

in Ghana,
in Cuba,
in Palestine.

I'm from all the North Philly classrooms and play-
    grounds I taught in, the ones that raised me as an
    adult.
The ones I created with the youth over at the old PAL
    on 10th and Pike.
And a little further south towards Kensington in what
    has now become an abandoned school building.

I am that queer person with a Bronx accent and
    washed up Tims.
The one who jumped into the fight as soon as I saw the
    pot boil over itself.
The one who burned incense and rubbed eucalyptus
    lotion between our palms.
So we can remember to breathe. So we can remember
    to feel. So we can remember who we are.

And today. Who am I?
A doctor who prescribes deep breaths and honest con-
    versations. A grower who shares the food and herbs
    I grow out of boxes and dresser drawers. A dreamer
    who knows that in order to free people from the
    shame of hunger I once felt, we must also free the
    land. An **organizer** who believes we can create
    safety without police and prison, without creating
    more suffering.

I am a reminder that **healing**, much like freedom
    dreaming, is for the brave.
That you are so powerful, even when your heart is so
    afraid.

New York City, 2003, Uptown Bronx 6 Train

We had just left the 3rd Avenue 138th Street station when a group of youth holding chains and wire
hangers in their hands strolled into our car. They were
between nine and eighteen years old and presented as
cis boys playing up a macho performance. All seven of
them were loud as they cursed and cracked jokes on
each other. Based on how they spoke Spanish I had
guessed that they were Dominican. I was seventeen
and annoyed and on high alert. I watched one of them
hit the other with a broken TV antennae and almost
hit a stranger. I tried to bring my focus back to a conversation with my homegirl, but Tracy was watching
too. She looked at them with the face I had seen her

make when she was ready to fight. Out of the corner of my eye, I saw two of the older boys walk towards a man who was sleeping in between two people sitting on the train car. One of the boys shoved the man's folded arms that held his resting head. Then he said, "*You* tryna fight?"

The sleeping man didn't pick up his head from his resting arms until the other young person punched him in the side of his forehead. Hard. By the time he put his hands up to protect his face, the people next to him grabbed their bags and rushed off the seat. Within seconds, the rest of the youth proceeded to jump the man. He tried to push them off and fight back, but there were just too many of them. I watched in horror, angry that nobody tried to help him. I was paralyzed by the fear that this man would get badly hurt right in front of me and that I, too, would get hurt if I jumped in and helped. And yet, I wanted so badly to help.

Then, two young girls, both who might have been cis and about fifteen years old, swooped in from the other side of the car. The adults watched the brawl and cleared the way for the swirling chaos of bodies. The girls pushed the boys away from the man, and eventually one girl was able to get in front of him and face the group. She kept pushing them away as she yelled, "What are you doing?! This is stupid! This man was minding his own business! Leave him alone!" At least two of them tried to push her away, but she was strong and was able to hold her ground and shove them back. Several train stops passed as they exchanged threats, breathing heavily from the adrenaline of the fight. Eventually they stopped arguing, but they each stood in their corners, staring the other down. The standoff came to an end ten minutes later when the boys got out at Parkchester. Tracy and I got off two stops later at Zerega Avenue. I was wildly inspired.

I walked off the train that day and asked myself a million questions:

Okay, but wasn't she afraid to get hurt?!
She took a couple hits, was she hurt?
Why did she put herself at such great risk for a stranger?
How did she become so brave?
Why didn't I do anything to help?
Could I ever be as tough as that young woman?
Why did they jump him?

Sometimes the questions to our answers are more important than the answers to our questions. Let me share a little bit more about my story and the history of where I come from so you can understand why I asked the questions I did.

Until I was three years old, I lived with my mother and grandmother in the Dewitt Clinton Housing Projects on 109th Street and Lexington Avenue in East Harlem, New York. My father was in my life every other weekend and on holidays, but my parents weren't married or in a relationship, which later in life, I was grateful for. The apartment in East Harlem was special because we were the first family in it and many people in our family lived in it at some point in their life. Living in that ground-floor apartment with windows facing the dumpster and the playground felt like a rite of passage.

In the late 1980s, Harlem had a huge crack and heroin problem. A lot of drugs were sold out of the mailboxes of our building. One of my earliest memories was walking into my grandmother's bedroom and seeing a man hunched over by the dumpster doing drugs of some kind. I screamed and scared us both.

Later, I would learn that the New York Police Department had been supplying many drug dealers, making money from so many people numbing their pain by smoking crack cocaine.[5] During this time a lot of factory jobs that belonged to Black and Brown people were leaving cities like New York, Philadelphia, Detroit, etc. This meant people were also out of work and in a lot of pain since they were struggling to pay bills and survive. Drugs numb pain. Since mostly Black and Brown people lived in Harlem, racist stereotyping allowed police to get away with this. In fact, most folks still don't know this history of policing and drugs, and how this impacted and affects the area to this day.

Living on the ground floor and very close to the lobby and front entrance of an eighteen-floor building meant that my family and I were close to a lot of drug and police activity. The day my mother found heroin needles near the sandbox I was playing in, she decided she wanted to leave. My mother saved enough money to move us to an apartment in Throggs Neck, a suburban part of the Bronx, when I was three. Still, every weekend we were back in East Harlem visiting family to celebrate birthdays, holidays, go to church, or walk 3rd Avenue to do food shopping or just window shop.

In the 1990s, East Harlem and Throggs Neck were two different worlds that were literally Black and white. In East Harlem, La India and Queen Latifah blasted out of boomboxes on top of people's shoulders or on top of a folding table selling socks and sunglasses. Right above that music was a chorus of police sirens. If I was sleeping over at my cousin's house on 109th Street, gunshots were a part of that. Tenement buildings were small and often overflowing with people, but still not as many people as those living in the

---

[5] Leonard Levitt, *NYPD Confidential: Power and Corruption in the Country's Greatest Police Force* (New York: St. Martin's Press, 2009).

tall housing projects that my family inhabited. Graffiti and murals painted along the sides of buildings told stories of people playing dominoes, *bomba y plena*, of Big Pun and Biggie and other young people who died young and hard. Throggs Neck was much more suburban with lots of row houses and trees. East Tremont Avenue was full of hair salons, restaurants, and bars that also had graffiti-style murals telling different stories. They outlined the Italy that its neighbors left behind; an angry Leprechaun ready to fight for Irish pride. Throggs Neck was quiet, but not that quiet and not that nice. There was also the occasional swastika graffitied on the walls to remind you that **racism** was welcome here.[6]

As I got older, I realized that where there were more **resources**, there was less violence. Often, this meant that where there were **resources** was wherever white people lived. I rarely saw fights in the Catholic private school I went to in the Bronx, but when I went to public high school in Manhattan, I saw fights every day. At Villa Maria Academy, we had a large field connected to a small slab of concrete overlooking the ocean. However, at High School for Health Professions and Human Services down on 15th Street in Manhattan, we were one of three schools stuffed into a single building. Classes sometimes took place in the lunchroom or the principal's office since there wasn't enough space. Much like the people who refused to help that man getting jumped on the train, over time, I accepted violence as a fact of life. Even at the Catholic school in the Bronx, my entire seventh-grade class made up a game called, "Kill the

---

[6] Swastikas were originally spiritual symbols of well-being for much of the world. In the 1930s, German Nazis reversed the meaning and used it as a symbol to belittle and instill fear in Jewish people as they engaged in genocide.

Carrier." The point of the game was to catch the ball and outrun the entire grade. Whoever had the ball was subject to getting punched, kicked, smacked, or thrown down to the ground.

So, while violence was not new to me, watching those two girls on the train jump in to defend an adult from a whole group of boys was nothing I had seen before. The questions I had asked myself that day—about why those boys jumped that man and why those girls jumped in—stayed with me.

Leaving Home and Questioning All of My Answers

As I got older and studied and traveled outside of the Bronx, I was exposed to hard truths about the history of this country. Community violence did not happen in the hood because Black and Brown or poor people were naturally more dangerous. The lack of **resources** like quality education, housing, work, and healthcare created dangerous **conditions** and very few choices. That is the despair that **oppression** creates.

Take a breath with me dear one. The breath can ease the heart when we hear hard things. I want to go back to my story and how it led to this book, but before I do, I want to dig a little deeper into what **oppression** means. Hopefully it will also help you to think about what I meant earlier when I said this book is about offering stories and tools for creating emotional and political freedom.

Learning about the history of **oppression** helped me to understand the roots of poverty and violence, and why it felt more common in places like East Harlem and certain parts of the Bronx. **Oppression** is the combination of **privilege, prejudice**, and **power**. This creates a system that benefits some people by harming others or at the expense of another group of people. Let's take a second to break that down through an example we can visualize in our minds.

I like to think about the movie *Finding Nemo*. Nemo is a young fish who lives in the open sea with his family, until he is captured by humans and sold to a pet store. He winds up in an aquarium in a doctor's office but will eventually be given as a gift to the doctor's niece, Darla. The other fish in the aquarium warn Nemo that Darla is known for being rough and killing her fish. Nemo is supposed to replace a fish she had just killed.

The open sea that Nemo lives in represents the free world that many people believe the United States to be. **Oppression** in this example can be represented by the different levels of society—the level of business and the level of family. In this case, it's the fishermen and pet store owners, and the dentist and his niece. They used their **privilege, prejudice**, and **power** as humans to benefit themselves at the expense of Nemo and other fish like him. They take Nemo away from his family, make money from selling him, and place him in the care of a child who finds joy in causing deadly pain. There are no consequences for her behavior.

Oppression is like the water inside of a large fish tank. A fish tank is usually made of clear glass, which makes you think you are a part of a free world, but the glass—much like **institutions** such as school and government—can make the world feel smaller for those with less institutional **power** and less **privilege**. This includes poor people, queer and **trans** folks, people with disabilities, and people of color, especially Black folks.

Oppression is in the waters that we breathe and swim in, which is why it can be hard to identify. We may not always see how that water makes us sick. Or stuck. You don't know what you don't know. Oof! Deep and a little bit scary, right?

Connect back with the breath in case it has gotten short or shallow.
Check in with yourself.
Consider the possibility that this book offers some real-life examples and tools about creating brave spaces to name and heal ourselves from the waters we swim in. And know this: we can't change anything we haven't named first.

The sad truth is that there are many systems and levels of **oppression**. **Racism, sexism, heterosexism, transphobia, capitalism, imperialism** are all examples of **oppressive** systems. These systems are based on beliefs of superiority for a person's race, gender, **sex, sexuality,** financial status, and where they were born. We will talk more about these in Chapter 1. You can also peek at pages 34–36 if you can't wait.

Institutions like school, hospitals, government, housing, and business are places where different levels of **oppression** impact people's lives. For example, **institutional oppression** looks like public schools in neighborhoods where there are mostly Black and Brown kids receiving less money than private schools because they receive their funding based on the property taxes, which are based on how the banks determine how much they and the housing are worth. Since slavery ended, the government has not put attention and **resources** where Black and Brown people live, particularly areas where folks are not offered quality jobs.

The banks and real estate have mimicked a similar attitude. Even until this day, they have determined the land is worth less where Black and Brown people have lived. This is also known as **redlining**. As a result, these schools are often overcrowded, have more cops than counselors, and have very few Black and Brown teachers. Children in these schools often don't learn much of their historical contributions to world history or question why things are the way they are. They are not fed nutritional and tasty food that supports their brains' development or how they feel in their bodies.

Most schools also force students to fit themselves into the **gender binary**, despite many cultures throughout history having many **genders**. That includes the **Indigenous people** of this country where some folks identify as two-spirit.[7]

"Girls line up on this side for recess and boys line up here."

"Boys go to room 103 for health class and girls go to room 305."

This leaves no room for **nonbinary** students to have a place, and it also creates an environment where **nonbinary** and **trans** students are more vulnerable to judgment, violence, and being disconnected from the school body.

How do you think all of this will affect how children feel about themselves as students or as people? Some of you reading this already know how it feels, because you are these children. If this is you, please know that **institutional oppression** may try and trick you into **internalized oppression**, which is when we begin to believe negative things about ourselves and the people that look like us. Knowing this can help you challenge negative **self-talk**. Please know that there are other trustworthy adults and **resources** to help you, and it may require some real intentional work on your part to find them and allow them in to support you.

---

[7] Two-spirit refers to someone who sees themselves as both masculine and feminine, or a third gender. There are different words for this depending on the culture and language of an Indigenous nation.

However, without addressing the painful experiences **oppression** creates, our hearts can begin to harden. We can start believing that our **power** lies in how we can control and conquer people without mercy. Violence destroys our imagination. It can push us to stop believing in ourselves and stop trusting people or believe that change in their situation or in the world is impossible.

Much like those boys who jumped that man on the train for simply existing, **interpersonal oppression** is about the way that people will use the little bit of **power** they have to **harm** others with less **power** for their own interest. Often in the inner city, there is a mindset that, no matter your **gender**, if you are violent then you are seen as tough. If you are tough, then you are seen as real. If you are real, then you are safe.

Figure 0.1: Interrupting interpersonal violence on the 6 train, c. 2003. Illustration by Pascal Ife Williams (2023).

Creating a TUFF Girls for All the Tough Girls

Are you tough?
What does being tough mean to you?
Has your definition changed over time?

As a tween or a teen, I didn't think I was tough at all. I was pretty strong and athletic since I was involved with sports and dancing. I drew confidence in being physically aggressive with boys who disrespected girls, especially if they were one of my friends! But I really wasn't a fighter. I was a pretty chill and social kid, whether at school or the community center I attended.

Although, when I was in the second grade, I physically bullied a girl by hitting her during recess simply because I thought it was fun. Her friend would try and intervene, but she wound up getting punched on by me until she finally told the teacher. I'm glad now that she stood up for herself, since neither she nor her friend deserved to be a punching bag. My doing that to them was definitely "**fake tough**." The other reason I felt I was **fake tough** at that age was because there were plenty of other moments when I didn't feel very confident when it mattered, like when teachers belittled me or when adults touched me inappropriately.

As I got older and became more concerned about the safety and equity of Black and Brown communities, including my own, my definition of tough changed. It was not just about how much violence your body had taken. It was asking tough questions like the one Malcolm X asks, "Who taught you to hate yourself?" Tough was about growing new muscle to love myself even when I struggled with family and community—to stretch myself even more to still hold people in compassion. Being tough asked me to look outside the window of my own pain at all the wars happening in the world and refuse to lose hope.

Just as I was starting TUFF Girls, I was also just starting to learn about **community organizing** through a national organization I helped to start in 2013 called the Black Youth Project (BYP) 100. We were organizing through a **Black queer feminist lens**. Watching and learning **organizers** from different social **movements** care about a just world for all Black people changed my life. I realized it takes a certain kind of toughness to face injustice without causing more **harm**. From **land** and **housing justice** to the fight against **climate change**, I have learned that people have jumped into the fight like the young women on the train in many different ways and for a very long time.

TUFF Girls for a Tough World

I started TUFF Girls in 2014 because I wanted to create a safe space for Black and Brown **femmes** to reflect on our pain and **power**. As I shared earlier, TUFF stands for Turn Up for Freedom. In TUFF Girls, we said that you are owed the space and room to not have to be tough, to feel safe enough to simply exist and to have access to all of your feelings without judgment. We also said you deserve the truthful versions of history and the political education to understand the root causes of violence. That included recognizing the **intersectionality** of **oppression**.[8] That's just

---

[8] See Kimberle Crenshaw, "Demarginalizing the Intersection of Race and Sex: A Black Feminist Critique of Antidiscrimination Doctrine, Feminist Theory, and Antiracist Politics" (1989), in *Feminist Legal Theory*, ed. Katharine T. Bartlett and Rosanne Kennedy (New York: Routledge, 1991), 58.

a fancy word that means that pain is shaped by more than one **oppression**: **racism**, **sexism**, *and* **classism**. The term was created by **Black feminist** Kimberle Crenshaw and was based on the lived experiences of Black women. We will get to more words like these words for forms of **oppression** in the next chapter.

For over five years, TUFF Girls would continue to evolve as a brave space where Black and Brown (mostly Puerto Rican and Dominican) middle and high school cis girls built bonds with each other as they discussed **anti-Black racism**, **sexism**, **transphobia**, and **class struggles** in their community. The hope was to have **trans** girls in our program. Despite this being in our mission statement, we did not come across girls who identified as **trans** in our neighborhood, which was where recruitment efforts were focused. It's possible these girls also did not feel safe to identify as **trans** or comfortable being in a program that was dominated by cis girls. It was a limitation in our program that we should have spent more time addressing. If you are cis and gathering girls, I hope you learn from our mistakes.

We held our meetings in a dance studio inside of a community center in North Philadelphia, as well as in two other community organizations, including a farm, in the same section of the city. For anyone who lives in the city of Philadelphia, North Philadelphia or "North Philly" is known for its native-born rappers Meek Mill and the late PnB Rock and much of the economic struggles we hear about in their songs.

The goal for creating this brave space was to nurture the trust needed to share personal stories and begin to see the patterns in our different struggles. It was a space to learn political education, and that helped to explain these conditions and strategize ways to face it as a collective. TUFF Girls also had the opportunity and financial support to organize events for their communities in order to educate and mobilize them towards change.

It was fun, but it was work. While the girls enjoyed the emotional freedom they felt as they made up dances or sang freedom song chants, it was also hard for them to feel like they could make strides towards political freedom when they were still experiencing bullying from other cis girls, food and housing insecurity, losing loved ones to gun violence, or getting harsh disciplinary treatment from parents and schools. Building bonds within TUFF Girls was a challenge at times because of these very things.

In 2019, we took a year off to redesign TUFF Girls so that we could help schools create this kind of space for girls. Just as we were getting ready to roll out, COVID-19 shut down the city and the world. As much as I tried to imagine how to recreate TUFF Girls virtually, I simply couldn't. I had also started to question what it meant for me to be the face of a Black-led organization in Philadelphia given my light skin, educational and **class privileges**, and someone who was also not from Philly. Spirit said it was time for me to move out of the way so that TUFF Girls could complete its life cycle with grace.

In December 2020, with the support of our board, we made the hard decision to sunset TUFF Girls. A sunset is the intentional closing of a program. The goal for our sunset was to allow everyone involved to reflect on what made it special, what were the mistakes made, and the barriers we faced in the work. We also held grief and gratitude for what the space offered our lives.

This book is part of that process. Our hope is to share the lessons learned by TUFF Girls in this book, so that you have more tools to use as you organize your own spaces to heal and build **power**. We hope that as you gather the girls to this work, that you center those who are most impacted by **patriarchy** and **transphobia**.

Figure 0.2: Reading as a part of collective care. Illustration by Pascal Ife Williams (2023).

How This Book Is Organized

This book is organized around five leadership **principles** that were developed with Kerrin Lyons, née Simmons, another brave adult who got TUFF Girls off the ground with me in that North Philly community center in Hunting Park. The old PAL on 10th Street. We wanted a set of **principles** that would help our participants think about the leadership that was needed in the face of injustice that has gone on for too long, and that had a huge impact on our emotions and the way in which we see the world.

We sat around my kitchen table for close to four hours talking about our own experiences as young people. We remembered the great **organizer** of the civil rights **movement**, Ella Baker, and her ideas about group-centered leadership. We also thought about the political changes that our society needed. A small pile of ashes grew from all the sticks of incense that burned on during our conversation. Each **principle** was connected to each other as if they held onto each other and formed a full circle:

- **Healer of self**
- **Protector** of your sister
- **Scholar-activist** of our history
- **Organizer** of our people
- Turnt Up for **Radical Joy**[9]

These were leadership **principles** that invited Black and Brown girls to consider their **power**—mind, body, and spirit. It thought about her as an independent person who was also a part of a community. It thought about leadership and building **power** for individual *and* collective freedom. Her inner world *and* her outer world.

To be a **healer of self** was a **principle**, which recognized that we live in a world full of **trauma** that is often unspoken. **Trauma** is an event or historical process that has a long-lasting impact on you emotionally, mentally, and physically. Reflecting on your own story, and how **trauma** and **systems of oppression** work, helps you in discovering your voice. Understanding how to process and manage our mental and emotional health helps us stop the circular nature of violence. Or, as some people call it, "when hurt people hurt people."

---

[9] This principle was initially called "Turnt Up for Life." Over the years we found while this one sounded exciting, it usually required some additional explaining in order to be clear. In 2019, when we were reviewing changes to the program, the board decided to rename this principle "Radical Joy."

To be a **healer** prepares you to be a better **protector** of your own humanity and someone else's. For a TUFF Girl to be a **protector** challenged this belief of **patriarchy** which said that "boys/men" are our natural **protectors**. This **principle** recognized that keeping each other safe and standing up for people who are victims of injustice was the job of everyone, including youth leaders. It also supported principled struggle with peers and friends, but it was also about protecting the communities we are growing up within.

The third **principle** is to be a **scholar-activist** of our history, present, and future. It is understood that to be a **healer of self** and **protector** of others we are called to **study** the story behind our hurt and why girls and **gender-expansive** youth endure the pain that they do. Practicing this **principle** allows us to understand the **principle** of being an **organizer** of responding to a collective need or in times of conflict or injustice. This might look like organizing a peace circle on the playground during recess when two girls are ready to fight or joining a student-led march demanding for more counselors than cops.

The last **principle**, to be turnt up for **radical joy**, recognizes that because of the **trauma** and violence experienced at a young age or having to take on adult responsibilities some kids have had to grow up sooner. This **principle** recognized that our joy was a source of our **power**, and it always has been. Fun and hope is not just some "little kid stuff." For Black and Brown girls, and especially girls growing up in communities where there is a lot of violence, play and joy create another reality when your world feels unsafe and unloving. That, in itself, is an act of self-preservation to honor.

Practicing these **principles** were ways we re-imagined being tough and doing the work towards individual and collective freedom.

How Should Someone Read This Book and What Can They Expect?

I encourage you to listen to your gut as you read this book. You know what you need and what you are ready to read and process. Although the **principles** build on each other, you can very well jump to the **principle** that speaks to you. If we keep with the earlier example in which the **principles** are like a circle holding hands with each other, imagine yourself in the middle of that circle. You may jump from different chapters as you feel inspired. As you finish each chapter, I encourage you to come back to the middle of that circle. Always come back home to yourself to see how what you read feels in your body. Read at a pace that feels right for you and what you are currently experiencing. This will help the book feel like an honest and gentle guide for where you are in your own journey of life. Each chapter is broken down into three big sections.

Section 1: The Her-Story

I start each chapter with a story from TUFF Girls so that you can see the **principles** in action. Trust me when I say we were never perfect in practicing these **principles**. We often don't get to read about the ways Black and Brown girls are **healing** and organizing, especially when they are from the hood. These stories are about how we practiced the **principles** in the conditions we were in. Yours might be different, so they may look different. These stories aren't instructions, they are more like inspirations for your imagination.

Additionally, since TUFF Girls only consisted of cis girls, keep in mind that the **principle** in action may look different for **trans** girls. For example, the

principle of **healer** spoke to the ways we were **healing** together from **systems of oppression**. The system of **transphobia** doesn't impact cis girls in ways that it does for **trans** girls, so the **healing** work will be different.

Section 2: The Hard Facts

To help break down the **principles** in more detail, I then provide some more research and background information so that you can feel more informed about how this **principle** is relevant to communities *outside* of my own experience and that of TUFF Girls. I'm not going to lie, at moments it may feel like you are in a Social Studies class. When I taught Social Studies and we were about to get into the lesson I would say, "Let's get into it!" I will say that here in the heading so that you know we are switching gears. While I would love it if you read this section of the chapter closely, there is no judgment if you need to skim this in the beginning.

Section 3: The Gentle Reminders and Tools

Lastly, you will find reflection questions and/or activities for you to consider how to practice on your own. Take what works and leave the rest. Each chapter will close with other readings you might enjoy, as well as a playlist to jam to as you reflect on the **principle**. And lastly, there will be a glossary for bigger words and concepts. Every word in **bold** can be found in the dictionary. Just remember, these words and concepts are likely just new language for an experience your body already knows.

Who Is This Book For?

This book is for folks who don't consider themselves a "reader" and for those who do. If you are curious and maybe even a little anxious about awakening collective **power**, then this is definitely for you, my friend. Most importantly, it is for youth who feel themselves to be a girl. It is for those who like to dress masculine or feminine or both; it is for those whose private parts may not match up with who they feel themselves to be; and it is for those who may like other girls or other boys or nobody at all. It is for those who are also questioning their **gender**.

I was thirty-six years old before I realized that I was **nonbinary**. My **gender** was not that of a girl/woman or a boy/man. It was more like the ocean, where every day the tide was different. Today, and most days, I feel like a lady boi. For years, students called me Ms. Mari and eventually Dr. Mari. However, as a way to honor the fullness of myself, I went back to a childhood nickname and I ask them, and I ask you, to call me Dr. E. Dr. E feels like a homecoming.

Whether you are in middle or high school and wish you had a brave space to build with people, or if you are already in a club or on a team and want to strengthen your bond and ability as a crew to make change—this book is meant to make you feel less alone. You might also keep to yourself and avoid being with groups of girls because you have had negative experiences with them. This book is for you too. Those experiences were real. This book can help give you the tools to imagine and slowly create a community that is a true support system. It starts first with a nice deep breath, and the very first principle of leadership: to be a **healer of self**.

CHAPTER 1

HEALER

When we choose to heal, when we choose to love, we are choosing liberation. This is where all authentic activism begins.

—bell hooks

The biggest thing I learned [in TUFF Girls] was calming techniques. We are coming from North Philly, there was nothing calm about that. Meditation, doing yoga, protecting my energy, and staying sane. I didn't see that nowhere else. Even though I was resisting in the beginning, it served me later on. It gave me the tools to stay sane in the real world.

—Nyjah Smith, TUFF Girls Leader

It was the energy of TUFF Girls that made it special.

—Shari Cain, TUFF Girls Leader

Practicing Being a Healer in TUFF Girls: Redefining Leadership

As you walked closer to a TUFF Girls space—whether it was at the community center or in the woods—you would probably smell Egyptian Musk incense burning or palo santo. This cleared the air and the mind and inspired the body to take a deeper breath in case you forgot.

Music would be playing, usually some new R&B or hip-hop artist, or an old-school one like Queen

Latifah who talked a lot about women's empowerment. This brought the fun and told the body you had
permission to move and dance here and feel respected
by the lyrics.

Depending on the community center we were
in, we either sat on yoga mats, or couches, or chairs,
and always in a circle. This made us feel like equals,
whether you were a TUFF Girl, a teaching assistant/
staff, a parent, or myself. As the founder and director of a youth-led space, it was one important way to
show my commitment to sharing **power**.

Up on the wall was the **agenda** for the day, the list
of our **principles**, and a list of community agreements
we came up with together on day one. This helped us
be clear on how we were using our time and why we
were there in the first place. It was a visual reminder
of our commitment to making this a safer space and
a brave space when conversations got tense or hard.

Whether it was pizza or snacks, there was always
food. This was the fuel our bodies needed for all the
thinking and feeling ahead of us. We were as consistent as possible with aromatherapy, music, our circle,
our visuals, and our food because consistency helps
the brain and heart trust the space. We tried to do this
even when we were not in our typical meeting space
in the community center, but at a march in downtown
Philly or at a hiking trail in a more suburban part
of the city. "The space" is not just a physical one. As
Luzsil once said in a public conversation that TUFF
Girls led at the Black Girl Project conference in
Brooklyn in 2016: "For me, sisterhood is a safe space.
The way we create that trust with each other to tell
each other anything and to really listen to each other."

"Have you ever been on a plane?"

I would ask this question to girls and their mam-
mas, aunties, grandmamas—or whichever adult they
brought with them in order to learn more about

TUFF Girls. We would be sitting on their porch. Or on the front steps on 10th Street. Sometimes we gathered around a table in the dance studio inside the rec center. About half of them hadn't flown on a plane, about half had, and all of them were curious about where I was going with this.

Every single time you board an airplane several flight attendants stand in the middle of the aisle and review with all the passengers what to do if there is an emergency while in the air. The flight attendants show you how to find and grab the oxygen mask above your seat and then tell adults with small children to put their mask on before putting one on their little ones.

"Why do you think that is?"

The most common answer they gave was the one I was looking for:

"Because if the mama tries to put her baby's mask on without putting on her mask first, all that smoke can kill her."

* * *

In TUFF Girls, we wanted to help middle school and high school students (and their families) name how **oppression** and violence was like that smoke, robbing them of breath, one of their greatest **powers**. Taking care of yourself and paying attention to your **healing** journey was like putting on an oxygen mask— you did it not only so that you can breathe, but so that when you are in relationships with others, you could help them breathe too. The **power** you have to make choices in a situation is also known as **agency**. Remembering your **agency** in hard situations is about using the **resources** inside of you (like the breath) and outside of you (like community) in order to get that **power** back after it feels robbed.

In my experience teaching in a working-**class** school in North Philly, the conversation about leadership had mixed messages about **agency**. It was about how well you listened or performed a task or won a thing. At TUFF Girls, we weren't interested in repeating the ways that the media or even some adults shouted AT young people about personal responsibility and playing by the rules.

"Real leaders are always on time and ready for school and always listen to adults in charge!" Yes, being on time and following rules helps you achieve personal goals for learning. Following rules, like not bringing guns to school, keeps everyone safe. All of that is very important, no question. But only talking about leadership when talking about your time management and "being a good kid" felt like asking young people for complete obedience without seeing them as humans who grieve, experience hunger or **anxiety**, or become targets for violence. It doesn't acknowledge that some adults in charge can be racist, sexist, homophobic, transphobic, or just plain abusive.

"Real leaders sacrifice everything in order to win and always outperform everyone!" This felt like a good way to stress everybody out, and to even encourage youth and adults to judge and bully others with a false sense of superiority. When we focus only on the outcome, and never reflect on the process, we lose a lot of lessons that making mistakes can teach us. It can encourage us to be superficial and overly concerned with our **ego**. Ah, the **ego**—that part of you that wants to be perfect. All of these myths about "real leadership" were not only false, but they were also the opposite of **healing**.

Healing was the first **principle** of leadership because at TUFF Girls we believed the goal of individual leadership was not about trophies. It was about individual *and* collective freedom. It was the first

principle because we knew from our own experiences as Black and Brown people, there were a lot of things in our media and visual images around us that unplugged us from our true **power**. In a society that equates money with **power** and whiteness with purity, there were a lot of shameful messages we heard about folks who weren't financially rich or white. These were the daily messages on our screens or in our ears that tried to convince us: what we look like or what we have is more important than who is inside.

But it's a lie! These messages encourage us to have a dishonest relationship with the truth of who we are as a person and as a people, especially if our schools are not offering us the space to learn our history and the history of this country.

This chapter will offer some of our big lessons we taught in TUFF Girls to help youth and adults understand what we were all **healing** from as a village. Even as a Doctor of Education, even with all the work I have done with myself: I am not an expert on **healing**. Let that be its own lesson. Your **healing** will be as unique as you are and it will also change over time. Use what makes sense for you and leave what doesn't.

From Philly to the Chi: The Chicago International Youth Peace Movement Conference

In Spring 2015, TUFF Girls was invited by a Chicago rapper and **activist** to attend the Chicago International Youth Peace **Movement** Conference. Representatives of TUFF Girls were chosen based on an application where they nominated other girls and explained why. Sameera Sullivan, Jazcitty Muniz, and Nyjah Smith were chosen as our TUFF Girls reps through this collective peer-nomination process. For each of them, it was their first time traveling to Chicago. Chicago is similar to Philadelphia in that it was a city where Black people gravitated to during the Great Migration of the 1930s to try and escape racial violence in the South. Instead, they found a new racial violence in Northern cities like Philly and Chicago, where they were forced to live in poor-quality housing and work in large factories run by racist bosses. Years of continued government neglect and policing of Black people in these cities has contributed to them becoming cities with high crime rates. By 2015, some were calling Chicago "Chi-Raq" and Philadelphia "Killadelphia." It's one thing for TUFF Girls to have read about this, but this conference was an opportunity to see with their own eyes. Reflecting about her experience in our sunsetting process, Nyjah said that learning about the impact of violence, and the kind of peace work that people in Chicago and nationally were doing to address it, offered her a deeper sense of empathy for herself and for her community back home.

Figure 1.1: Jazcitty, Sameera, and Nyjah at the Chicago International Youth Peace **Movement** Conference of 2015.

Let's Get Into It: Finding a Life Jacket in the Deep Waters of Oppression

Talking about **oppression** and injustices that have existed for a long time can feel as heavy as we might imagine the weight of the ocean to be, so let's just take a breath to get us started. How does that sound? Deep breath in, deep breath out. We are about to break down different **systems of oppression** even further than we did in the Introduction. Reading this might bring up some painful or uncomfortable experiences your body has experienced or you have heard about from others. Some of the names of these systems are also long and may be hard to say. Lean into the fact that you are simply learning a new vocabulary for something you most likely have already experienced or seen.

Each system of **oppression** touches on a different part of a person's identity such as their age, race, **class**, **gender**, sexual orientation, religion, place of origin, ability, body size, etc. A person's beliefs and attitudes about these categories that support unequal **power** differences are what **powers** a system. Unequal **power** differences are also known as a **power dynamic**. For example, a small child and an adult are two different people who both have the **power** to express themselves. However, a small child cannot work, does not have their own money or the lived experience to understand how the world works. An adult can do those things. They have **privileges** because of that dynamic. They move around independently in the world, and people will listen and trust that adult more. More **privilege** means more **power** and more responsibility. Being irresponsible and violent with **privilege** and **power** keeps **oppression** in place.

Sadly, these **systems of oppression** expose people to **trauma**. **Trauma** is the impact of a negative event or process that continues to last even after the event is over. Examples of **trauma** can include physical acts of violence like being hit or being jumped or even having to watch physical acts of violence or just hearing about it. It can include negative events that are less physical and more verbal, such as shaming someone or being told, "You will turn out just as bad as your mother/father." Most often, it is more emotional and less visible, like neglect. It can also be a historical process such as slavery.

What can make it hard to understand is that it is different for each person. What is traumatic for one person won't be traumatic for the other. A teacher can yell at a classroom of children, "You are acting like animals and you will never make it in life!" One student can be angered and feel motivated to prove them wrong. Another student can laugh, but in reality, really take that comment in and start to believe that about themselves. Sometimes when a kid is acting out or "being bad" or even being very quiet in class, they are actually showing the symptoms of **trauma** from within and outside of school. When **trauma** is not addressed or processed, and it often isn't, it will continue to impact our emotions and even the choices we make. Some symptoms can include:

- Difficulty focusing
- Trouble with remembering things
- Feeling anxious or restless and unable to keep still
- Sadness that is hard to explain
- Anger and even rage
- Difficulty feeling safe or trusting
- Difficulty sleeping or sleeping all the time
- Nausea
- Feeling empty
- Not wanting to live

When these symptoms last and the child and the adults are not trying to address the root issues, it can encourage the body to protect itself in ways that are not always healthy. Some of the behaviors we can see include:

- Falling behind on schoolwork or not wanting to go to school at all.
- Hitting or verbally attacking when you sense there is danger/threat.
- Mindlessly scrolling through a phone or playing video games for long periods of time.
- Engaging in sexual activity, fighting, or using drugs/alcohol to numb pain/problems.

Much like oceans in the real world can overlap, so do various **systems of oppression**. Let's go back to the example of the child and the adult and think about a real-life example in a classroom. In 2019, Kaia Rolle was a six-year-old Black girl who loved to sing and dance, according to her grandmother. One day at school, she was having a temper tantrum in class when she kicked a teacher. School resource officer Dennis Turner, who had been called into the class, decided to arrest her and bring her to a juvenile detention center, where she was fingerprinted. Her grandmother tried to explain to Officer Turner that she had a lack of sleep because of her sleep apnea which has led to behavioral problems. The officer then said that he had sleep apnea and doesn't act like that. Right, Officer Turner, you don't act like that because you are an *adult* with sleep apnea, not a child!

In this example, we see a Black girl being treated like both an adult and a criminal for normal behavior of small children with a health challenge. The fact that no other adult stopped the officer from arresting Kaia shows how common our society's beliefs about Black children are.

Table 1.1: Different systems of oppression and the power dynamics they create between groups of people.

System of Oppression	Powered by Belief In	Power Differential	Examples
racism	anti-Blackness; white supremacy	Benefits white people at the expense of **BIPOC** (Black, Indigenous, people of color).	Most K–12 schools require children to read less books written by **BIPOC** authors. Schools justify this by saying they require students to read "the Classics," typically written by white men.
colorism	white supremacy	Benefits lighter-skin **BIPOC** at the expense of darker-skin **BIPOC**.	Associating lighter skin or European features on people of color or Black folks as more beautiful and associating dark-skinned features as less than beautiful.
sexism	patriarchy	Benefits masculinity/men at the expense of **femmes/** women and **gender-** nonconforming people.	Although women make up the majority of teachers for K–12, they are typically paid less than men with the same work experience.
classism	capitalism	Benefits rich people at the expense of poor people.	For many young teens, their first job is at a fast-food restaurant where they receive $7 or less per hour, and their wage doesn't increase as they get older. The CEO of a place like McDonald's is only able to make millions because their employees are paid low wages.

System of Oppression	Powered by Belief In	Power Differential	Examples
heteronormativity	**sexuality**	Benefits heterosexual people over queer communities.	For the schools that do offer comprehensive **sex** education, many of them only teach safe **sex** practices for heterosexual youth, since it assumes that young people are only engaging in heterosexual **sex**.
cisnormativity	**gender binary; transphobia**	Benefits **cisgender** people at the expense of **nonbinary** and **transgender** people.	In order for **cisgender** people who believe in the **gender binary** to be comfortable in schools, several states have a law which denies **trans** students at K–12 schools the right to use the bathroom that matches their **gender** identity. Bathrooms often become hidden places of violence.
colonialism	**Manifest Destiny; white supremacy**	Benefits colonizing countries at the expense of colonized countries.	We call colonizing countries the "First World" because of how it built its wealth on stealing land, **resources,** and people from the countries it colonized for centuries. This process of accumulation is called **colonization.**

System of Oppression	Powered by Belief In	Power Differential	Examples
ableism	able-bodied privilege	Benefits people without physical, mental, and emotional disabilities at the expense of those who do.	Between 2015–2016, students with disabilities were arrested and physically harmed by school police at higher rates than nondisabled students. Students with disabilities were nearly three times more likely to be arrested than students without disabilities, and the risk is multiplied at schools with police.
Zionism	Israelis and those who identify as Jewish	Benefits Israelis at the expense of Palestinians to even exist.	While there is no official ban on Palestinian Americans traveling to historic Palestine, otherwise known as Israel, they are often turned away by Israeli officials or questioned for many hours based on the idea that they are a security threat. However, those with Hebrew names or who identify as Jewish are able to easily pass through Israeli customs.

Like water in a fishbowl, the fish, no matter how old they are, can find it hard to see. **Racism** and **sexism** are not the only systems that work together to make for harmful environments for people. There are many. On pages 34–36, you see a chart that breaks down **systems of oppression** and the beliefs that **power** them and the **power dynamics** between people. **Power dynamics** are the uneven levels of **power** between two groups of people. The examples hopefully help us understand what we are **healing** from, and the kind of **harm** that often goes unseen.

Let's Get Into It: Knowledge Is Power, Knowledge Is Healing

In TUFF Girls, political education looked a lot like learning the definitions of these systems. Here they are in a chart, but people have written entire books about them because of their wide impact on the history of people around the world. Some of those books are listed in the "Recommended Reading" section at the end of this chapter.

I remember one Thursday afternoon in Fall 2015, TUFF Girls were all sprawled out on yoga mats, some laying on top of each other. We were going over the definition of **white supremacy** when I asked the group, "What do you think the impact of **white supremacy** is on how Black people think about ourselves?" They were quiet.

They had heard of **racism**, which was often taught as a thing individuals did in the past. It's natural to get quiet when trying to understand something new, especially when someone is asking you to think about how it applies to your own life. Especially when you start thinking about how it might reveal something painful.

Suddenly, Anjelica, who was eleven at the time, jumped to her feet and said, "It makes us believe the lie that whiteness is better! And that lie can make us feel bad about who we are. It made me feel bad about who I am. And it's not right! It's not right at all." Anjelica had an aha moment. Her eyes were wide open as she said this, and the other girls agreed.

We can't start to heal if we are not willing to be real with ourselves when we receive new information. Being real is about going inward. Seeing the truth that lives there and being honest and compassionate with ourselves.

When we are real with ourselves, the way Anjelica was, it also inspires others to have the courage to do the same. She was able to go to a deeper and vulnerable place while also being compassionate. This was a leadership moment in **healing**. Her sharing encouraged others to reflect out loud about their own overcrowded schools. They were full of other Black and Brown children, which often felt full of chaos. They often felt like they weren't learning.

"A lot of kids come in with problems."

"A lot of teachers don't know how to deal with kids with problems."

"It's like we do the same worksheets over and over again."

When they saw schools on TV with white children, however, there was always lots of fun and much more creative learning happening. At first, they assumed that these were just natural differences. The kids in their schools were bad and the kids on iCarly were good, even when they made mistakes. This is also the belief of **white supremacy**: whiteness is naturally good and is the standard for normal.

But our conversations inspired them to zoom out and ask different questions. Instead of just focusing on student's behavior, they questioned why it seemed like their schools had less money for fun activities, or why their classrooms were old and dirty, why the food was so nasty, and why there were few books and technology but lots and lots of worksheets. This wasn't about making excuses for bad behavior. This was about naming the conditions that impacted *why* their peers made choices that weren't healthy.

They were able to see themselves and their peers not simply as bad kids, but as fish breathing and swimming in the water of **white supremacy**. This is the water that children and adults are all **healing** from even as we continue to live in it. Some die from it, like Aiyasha Stanley Jones, a seven-year-old girl shot by cops raiding her family's apartment. **White supremacy** is just one of many **systems of oppression** polluting it. Sadly, there is a physical impact on the brain and on the body from having to swim in these waters all the time.

That's a lot. I encourage you to take a nice deep breath. **Oppression** seeks to take our breath away, so we have to always remember the breath when it gets hard. This will keep us from drowning. It always has.

Breathing and swimming in these waters after many years can cause us to feel depressed, anxious, and even angry. The suicide rate for Black youth doubled from 2001 to 2017. Latina and Native American girls have some of the highest suicide rates among their peer groups. Without healthy models to deal or cope from the stress and suffering of these conditions, we become sad and angry and take out our frustration on the people closest to us—including ourselves.

> *Hurt people hurt people, as many will say.*
> *We can also say,* ***healing*** *people help people heal.*

So then, how do we heal? I can't answer that for you, for your **healing** journey is unique to the circumstances of your life. I can say the more time and attention you give that journey the clearer that answer becomes.

I can also say that for me, bell hooks and Audre Lorde taught me that first I had to name it.

Then, I had to feel it.

Eventually, I had to speak and write it out of me.

Doing that, I learned how to bring in people to feel it with me in safety and carry on with courage.

* * *

If it's true that knowledge is **power**, and I believe it is, then knowledge can be **healing**. Understanding that **oppression** is the root of violence can help you to not judge yourself and others so harshly or blame yourself for bad things happening to you. When **healing** is seen as a key **principle** of leadership it encourages you to reflect on how your environment impacts how you feel. It helps you to see the **agency**, or **power**, you have to manage your emotions so that they don't manage you. Being able to understand your **trauma**, your emotions, and your needs can give you the motivation to **demand** more than what you have been taught to accept as good, bad, or natural.

The beautiful thing about the brain, is that even though **trauma** can damage the circuits inside of it that help us be and feel healthy, when we support our body with the right activities and expose it to new environments, it can also begin to heal those circuits and build new ones. Scientists call this **neuroplasticity**. This is especially true when you are young.

Many of the tools and activities discussed in the next section can help you support the **healing** of your brain and your mind, body, soul. Many of these tools you can use on your own. Some of the other tools asked you to invite others into your nourishing.

That also means building trust, which takes time and instincts. Old pain can cloud our instincts, especially when **patriarchy** teaches:

- **Gender-expansive** people are not normal and are trying to be something they are not.
- Girls are emotional and cause too much drama.
- Girls are catty and boys make better friends.
- You are either a good girl or a bad girl.
- Boys hold more value, and we girls must compete for their attention and approval.
- Boys, and in particular Black boys, are violent.

One of our goals at TUFF Girls was to expose these myths and create new environments that said:

> *We see you. We see your pain and your brilliance, and we are willing to hold space for it.*
> *Because you deserve that, and so do I.*
> *It's the only way we have survived through hard times.*

No one can guarantee a completely safe space when gathering people. People are unpredictable. Plus, we are humans still carrying a lot of lies we have been taught about ourselves. We make mistakes, and we cause **harm**. When that happened in TUFF Girls, we would come back to our agreements, and revisit why our principle for **healing** was important. Here are other helpful reminders from when we focused on **healing** and practiced it in our community:

- You are not responsible for your **trauma,** but that doesn't give you permission to inflict **trauma** on someone else.
- Most of us are trying to be well in environments that are not well because of **oppression.**

- **Healing** is not always a feel-good process. On the other side of that emotional work is your **power**.
- More listening, less fixing. Sometimes, when someone shares a struggle they don't want advice or need someone to intervene. Sometimes they just want someone to listen and feel it with them.
- The goal is not to "get over it," whatever it is; the goal is to create a trustworthy space for yourself and others to *feel through it.*
- **Healing** is not just something that happens because of time. It is a lifelong choice that we make every single day, and it is a messy process that takes time, effort, and a lot of patience.
- Your choices shape your habits, and your habits shape your mindset. A mindset for **healing** based on your choices and habits is what helps you be a leader in creating **healing** spaces for others.
- **Healing** is not a straight line to success. You will take three steps forward and two steps back, and that's okay. That's normal. **Healing** is a lifelong journey.

What Else Are We Healing From?

Sadly, the people who look like us are often the people behind the violence we experience. One in four Black girls will experience sexual assault by eighteen years old. The majority of survivors will be related to or know the person who harmed them. It's not because *we* are bad people; unfortunately, many adults have not healed from all the violence they experienced as kids or continue to experience as adults. It's important that as survivors of violence we don't make excuses for them or blame ourselves. They have **healing** work that they have to do, and that is their responsibility.

And, society has a lot of work to do in order to make sure children and adults have their basic needs met.

- African American youth are 83 percent more likely than other youths to be without shelter; lesbian, gay, bisexual, and **trans** (LGBT) youth are a whopping 120 percent more likely to be without housing than other young people.[1]
- Food apartheid is the system of segregation where some groups of people have access to abundant, healthy food options and others do not. About 24 million Americans struggle under food apartheid, where it's difficult or impossible to access affordable and healthy food.[2]
- On a national scale, Black youth are more likely to enter and stay in foster care longer than their white counterparts. In Pennsylvania, 43 percent of Black youth were in foster care in 2016.[3]
- Parents of Black children are twice as likely to not have a job compared to white children.[4]

---

[1] Matthew Morton, Amy Dworsky, and Gina Samuels, *Missed Opportunities: Youth Homelessness in America, National Estimates* (Chicago: Chapin Hall at the University of Chicago, 2017), 12, https://voicesofyouthcount.org/wp-content/uploads/2017/11/ChapinHall_VoYC_NationalReport_Final.pdf.

[2] Leah Penniman, *Farming While Black: Soul Fire Farm's Practical Guide to Liberation on the Land* (Vermont: Chelsea Green Printing, 2018).

[3] Ryanne Persinger, "Pa.'s Black youth more likely to be in, stay in foster care: Report," *The Philadelphia Tribune*, November 13, 2018, https://www.phillytrib.com/news/pa-s-black-youth-more-likely-to-be-in-stay-in-foster-care-report/article_869247ef-175d-562a-af5d-d164854ef45c.html.

[4] Valerie Wilson, "Black Unemployment Is Significantly Higher than White Unemployment Regardless of Educational Attainment," *Economic Policy Institute*, December 17, 2015, https://www.epi.org/publication/black-unemployment-educational-attainment.

- One out of four cis Black women, by the time they turn eighteen, will have experienced sexual assault.
- Black girls are six times more likely to be suspended at school than their white peers.
- According to the Centers for Disease Control and Prevention's 2017 Youth Risk Behavior Surveillance survey: in the US, 10.5 percent of Latina adolescents aged 10–24 years attempted suicide in the past year, compared to 7.3 percent of white female, 5.8 percent of Latino, and 4.6 percent white male teens.[5]

---

[5] Laura Kann et al., "Youth Risk Behavior Surveillance – United States, 2017," *Surveillance Summaries* 67, no. 8 (June 15, 2018): 1–114, https://www.cdc.gov/mmwr/volumes/67/ss/ss6708a1.htm.

Tools for Practicing Being a Healer

This next section has tools, practices, and recipes for helping you as you experience stress, tension, and **trauma**. All of them can be used in community or as you take some space for yourself.

Breathwork

We can survive weeks without food, days without water, but only a few moments without our breath. We started this book by inviting you to take a breath. Bringing focused attention to the breath, to your inhale and your exhale, is the quickest way to be present to the here and now. It helps you to become mindful of what you are feeling, while also calming down intense feelings.

Breathwork looks and feels like many different things. The simplest kind of breathwork is to take a deep inhale through the nose while letting your belly rise, up towards your hands. Then, let a deep exhale out the mouth. Take a moment to check in. How do you feel?

Another one is square breathing. This looks like: inhaling for 1-2-3-4; holding the breath for 1-2-3-4; then, exhaling for 1-2-3-4. How does this feel?

In yoga, *pranayama* refers to the life force you feel in breathwork. There are specific kinds of breathing that come from that spiritual and cultural tradition. One of them is called "Lion's Breath." The Sanskrit name is *simha pranayama*. I love to do this one when I'm feeling a lot of aggression or feeling a lot of big feelings bottled up inside. Take a nice deep inhale through the nose, and then open your mouth wide as you exhale out the word, "ha!" and stick your tongue out. You may feel silly the first time you do this. Even in your giggles, you will likely feel it release tension.

Food

Healthy food and clean water are super important for both our physical and emotional health. Ever heard of being "hangry"? You know it: it's anger caused by hunger. The reality is, overly processed food with little nutrition, like instant ramen noodles, doesn't keep our battery charged up. In fact, too much processed food and sugar can make us sick, or make us feel depressed, anxious, and even tired.

The other hard reality is that many are going through it and just don't have the money or access to healthy food that tastes good. **Food racism** or "**food apartheid**" looks like majority Black or poor areas not having a grocery store with fresh veggies and fruits for miles, while richer areas where mostly white people live have much more access. **Activists** who engage in **food justice** work call this out, while also encouraging more access to healthy food to eat as well as whatever **resources** they need to grow their own food, much like our African and Indigenous **ancestors** did.

Growing from seed can be a very inexpensive way to always have access to veggies. The act of growing your own food can be very **healing** and provide you with the kind of food that will nourish your brain, your heart, your skin, and your insides. Worried about not having any land or space? A quick Google search using the words, "growing food in an apartment," will show you a list of tricks for how growing veggies and herbs in urban spaces is possible with a bit of creativity and patience.

Herbs

Harriet Tubman is most noted for her nineteen trips up and down the Underground Railroad route where she would help Black people escape slavery plantations in the South. She later became a spy for the Union during the Civil War. Most folks don't know that she was also a **healer** who understood the **power** and medicine of herbs. Many of our Black and Indigenous **ancestors** have a deep and spiritual relationship with the land. They carried so much wisdom about the **healing power** of herbs growing in the environment. European colonizers saw this wisdom as witchcraft while stealing the knowledge of plants and using that in combination with a medical science they were developing. Many of us were disconnected from this history and knowledge, but there were some who were able to preserve this wisdom and teach us what we know now.

Growing herbs or using plant medicine can also be really helpful ways to lift up our mood during depression, heal an upset stomach when we are sick or have **anxiety**, or offer relief from stress. We can use herbs to make tea, oils for our skin—for a **healing** bath, tincture, or a salve—or to burn. Do your own research before consuming, because some herbs are not meant to be ingested. You can also find a lot of dried and fresh herbs in most supermarkets or in a health food store.

But what's more powerful than growing your own medicine? Many herbs do well when grown inside and some even grow beautiful flowers. As you explore the different **healing** benefits of each herb, consider what you could see yourself growing in your room. Growing any form of life requires time and attention, but they call them "plant allies" or "plant helpers" for a reason.

Table 1.2: A list of herbal allies, also known as plant medicine, and their **healing** properties.

Herbs	Benefits
Chamomile	Calming effects; aids in sleep
Peppermint	Relieves indigestion, nausea, cramps, boosts mood
Ginger	Nausea, relief from menstruation, refreshes mood
Dandelion root	Renews the skin and will drive away the winter blues
Eucalyptus	Opens your lungs and helps you breathe
Jasmine	Enhances your mood and refreshes your skin
Lavender	Calms your nerves and rejuvenates your skin
Rose petals	Relaxes your body and refreshes your skin
Rosemary	Promotes relaxation and mental clarity
Lemon balm	Eases **anxiety**, tension, insomnia, nausea
Tulsi	Eases **anxiety**, lowers blood sugar levels, supports wound **healing**
Yarrow	Reduces fever, helps in setting **boundaries**, a "warrior's herb"
Mother's Wort	Supports emotional and physical heart through grief, supports healthy female reproductive system

Writing to Heal

Journaling is really great for three reasons: (1) it is complete freedom to express how you feel without worrying about how it sounds coming out; (2) the process of "writing it out" can help you to process something that is hard to think about; and (3), if you decide to burn it that can feel like a sweet release; OR, if you decide to keep it, then you have a record for the future of how far you have come. Here are some prompts that have been really helpful in hard moments:

> *What happened and how do I feel about it?*
> *What am I grateful for in this moment?*
> *What is the story about myself that I am creating right now? Is it based in fear or love? How can I rewrite it?*
> *If my best friend was feeling what I am feeling/ experiencing, what would I tell them?*
> *What are ten things that I love about myself? If that feels hard, what are ten things my close friends or family would say they love about me?*

Movement Exercises

Emotions are like balls of energy within us. Often, we have to move those balls of energy if we want to move our emotions, especially emotions like sadness, hopelessness, and even anger. Going for a walk (especially in nature), running, dancing it out, swimming, or even screaming can really support our nervous system. The "tapping technique," combines ancient Chinese acupressure and modern psychology where you tap different parts of your face with your fingers and say a mantra to help you work through worry.

These parts of your face, also known as meridians, are said to release certain energy and offer release. For a step-by-step guide to explore this technique, check out *The Tapping Solution for Teenage Girls* by Christine Wheeler.

Spiritual Exploration

When I was a young person, someone once described the different religions and spiritual practices of the world as many people discovering different ways to climb the same mountain. That made sense to me, especially since some religions and spiritual beliefs appeared to be on totally opposite sides of the mountains, but all of them were reaching towards some higher, more principled self. What side of the mountain have your people climbed? Does that walk or religion match up with your truth and how you understand how faith works?

As a child, I remember appreciating how the symbolism of walking up a mountain made me think about "walking by faith." When I think about the moments in my **healing** journey, where I also felt the most powerful, it was when I felt the most connected to a higher source. As a child who grew up in a Christian home this often looked like the protection I could feel when praying to God when I felt unsafe. When I became a teenager and felt depressed from heartbreaks, I would also write out my prayers and find comfort.

As I got older, I felt less spiritually connected to Christianity, especially after learning about the role it played in justifying **colonization** and slavery. In learning the history of my Black and Puerto Rican heritage before European colonizers robbed them of their culture, I felt much more spiritually grounded in an African spirituality. This recognized a higher **power** as well as the **power** of our enlightened **ancestors** and the existence of spirit guides. I'm also a practicing Buddhist who finds a lot of peace from chanting.

I share this because spiritual health can be important for helping us find strength and purpose. It can take some reflection and exploring to find a spirituality that lines up with your spirit. Where are you on that journey?

Yoga

Practicing yoga is another way that many people, including myself, see themselves climbing up the mountain toward their higher self. Yoga is becoming more popular as a kind of "gym class" in schools or recreation centers, but many locate the history of yogic traditions and spiritual practices that resemble yoga in ancient South Asia and ancient Egypt.

This practice focuses on breath, movement, and going inward to mediate. It is also a cultural practice connected to different spiritual philosophies. For some groups of people in South Asia, this included a body of spiritual and religious philosophies indigenous to different regions. Several South Asian spiritual leaders of this region brought yoga to the US to teach it. Westerners who had traveled to South Asia also brought it back to the US and made changes to make it fit within their culture. Many discussed the spiritual philosophy of yoga as seeing yourself as connected to all people through the Universe, or God, or Love.

You might see yoga happening in your school or community center and treated like a gym class. Practicing the physical poses can certainly increase strength, flexibility, and provide a greater sense of balance. But when we disconnect yoga from its cultural and spiritual origins, we engage in **cultural**

appropriation (or, the misuse of a cultural practice). We also miss out on the emotional and spiritual benefits it can have on our sense of self. Engaging with yoga as a practice of the mind, body, and spirit, and not just a physical one, can improve the way we show up as a more healed and whole-hearted human being. In other words, practicing yoga through its original purpose of connecting with our true spirit and with our sense of connection to other people, is how this **healing** art can help strengthen us to be the leaders of **social justice** that we need in our lives. Additionally, our breath is full of what yoga philosophers call "*prana* energy," or fire energy. This means that with intention and practice, our breath can serve as powerful medicine.

Dr. Sheena Sood, a yoga teacher who also taught yoga workshops in TUFF Girls, teaches us about decolonizing yoga. She points out that much of the original Indian teachings on yoga focus on individual liberation for privileged people, while also turning a blind eye to the violent **caste system** that discriminated against darker-skinned Dalit Indians.[10] This is a contradiction. Decolonizing yoga at the root pushes

---

[10] In her own words, she believes "that while yoga can be harnessed toward individual and collective liberatory purposes, it should not be romanticized as a naturally pure and peaceful practice. The traditions that we now know as yoga emerge from their own societies of **oppression** and inequality. Yoga emerged from a society that was ruled by an ideology of Brahminism for thousands of years. **Caste hierarchy** continues to plague Indian society and culture. For centuries, Brahmins, or the priests and ruler **class**, have governed how yoga has been taught to the masses. For instance, Brahmins often taught lower-caste people and Dalits that they are not godly or deserving of divine light because they were born into an impure caste, and that there is nothing they can do to change their status. We continue to see the influence of these harmful teachings of Brahmanism and Hindu supremacy in

us to not look away from **oppression**, but to breathe, and to stretch ourselves towards individual AND collective liberation. I invite you to consider this the next time you are on a mat or in tree pose.[11]

Therapy

I was eleven when my mom asked if I wanted to talk to a therapist. I told her no, but only because I thought that talking with a therapist meant that something was wrong with me. A lot of young people and adults refuse to see a therapist because they don't want to feel "crazy," or don't feel like talking about their problems with a stranger can help. In some cases, they may have heard of someone having a negative experience with a therapist or had a negative experience themselves.

When I finally did start seeing a therapist ten years later, I wish I had realized earlier how relieving it could be to share my pain with someone who was trained to listen to me with really careful ears. Not every therapist may feel like a good fit for you. I personally prefer a Black person or person of color therapist. But finding the right therapist is like finding the perfect pair of shoes: just because you don't find them in the first store you go to, doesn't mean you stop looking. Here are some other things to keep in mind when considering therapy:

---

how yoga is taught in India and in the US." Personal email communication with Dr. Sheena Sood on March 4, 2023.

[11] Dr. Sheena also invites folks to do this in a children's yoga program, Yoga Warrior Tales. To learn more about this program or see her writing on the need to decolonize yoga, check out her website at sheenashining.com.

- Finding the right therapist can take time. Don't give up if the first one isn't a good match for you.
- While talking to a stranger may feel weird at first, it is the one relationship where you don't have to worry about how what you are revealing is making them feel or feel pressured to ask how they are doing. You are allowed to be selfish here and just focus on you.
- Therapists don't fix your problems. They give you the space and the tools to help you face them with support. They can't live your life for you and they can't feel your feelings for you. As my first therapist, Dr. Tonya Ladipo, once told me, "You are the driver of the car, and I am in the passenger seat helping to give you directions if your car gets lost, gets stuck in a pothole, or breaks down. I can pass you the tools, but this is your car."
- The real work of therapy is not just in the session, it is how you apply what comes out of those sessions into your everyday life. This can mean making changes in how you normally approach a situation, which can also mean changes in your relationships.
- Therapy doesn't always feel good. That is not a bad thing, unless you feel like you are being judged or forced into an interaction you don't want. Sometimes when we are working through deep **traumas** like death or violence, it can bring back emotions we buried. When we return to these things and face them head on, we may have to relive traumatic emotions in order to be more free of them and their quiet hold on us.

Art Therapies

What do you think of when you think of someone going to therapy? For some folks, they may have an image of a person sitting on a soft couch as they talk about things that have happened with a person sitting across from them, listening and taking notes. In the movies, that person is the therapist, who is usually wearing eyeglasses. In real life, this is called "talk therapy"—they don't always wear glasses but they often do take notes.

Art therapies use talk therapy *and* different art practices in order to process traumatic events of life or big feelings like grief or sadness. This group of therapies include art therapy, dance/movement therapy, music therapy, and even drama therapy. These can be really helpful if talking about an event that is really difficult and you can't quite find the words to talk about it or your feelings.

Questions for Reflection:

1. One of the tools you have been invited to use as you read this book has been breathwork. If you tried practicing that, how has the experience been? If you decided to skip that, why do you think that is?

2. What are things in your life that are asking for attention and **healing**? How might your friends and family answer that question? Can you make a connection between this wound or wounds with one or more of the **systems of oppression** on the chart on pages 34–36?

3. What are some tools for **healing** you already practice? When you were reading through the tools, which ones made your body feel at ease and which ones made your body tighten up? Why do you think that is the case?

Recommended Reading:

Trans Teen Survival Guide, Fox Fischer and Owl Fischer

For Colored Girls Who Considered Suicide When the Rainbow Wasn't Enough, Nzotake Shange

Dear Teen Self: Tips to Help a Teenage Girl Navigate through Adolescence, Jaynay Chanel Johnson

How We Heal: Uncover Your Power and Set Yourself Free, Alexandra Elle

Daily Affirmations for People of Color, Iyanla Vanzant

The Black Girl's Guide to Healing Emotional Wounds, Nijiama Smalls

The Latina Guide to Health: Consejos and Caring Answers, Jane L. Delgado

Black Youth Rising: Activism and Radical Healing in Urban America, Shawn Ginwright

Black Girlhood Celebration: Toward a Hip Hop Feminist Pedagogy, Ruth Nicole Brown

Badass Black Girl: Quotes, Questions, and Affirmations for Teens, M. J. Fievre

Playlist for Healing:

"Free Mind," Tems

"Black Girl Soldier," Jamila Woods

"Holy," Jamila Woods

"River," Ibeyi

"Positivity," Beautiful Chorus

"I Am Enough," Beautiful Chorus

"Healing," BYP100 Choir

"Greatest Love of All," Whitney Houston

"Break My Soul," Beyonce and Big Freedia

"I Am Her," Shea Diamond

CHAPTER 2

PROTECTOR

The most disrespected person in America is the Black woman. The most unprotected person in America is the Black woman. The most neglected person in America is the Black woman.

—Malcolm X

I built a lot of friendships. With two people in particular, we came in as friends but we left as sisters. We've been stuck with each other ever since.

—Najah Whitehead, TUFF Girls leader

[In TUFF Girls], you got a sense of the closeness that was being built, and that was a powerful visual for the girls to see, especially Black girls who come from a low-income neighborhood. When we see it in the media we are already told how people are and how they don't engage with one another. So to see the tenderness and compassion and the community they were able to forge, even in their conflict with each other, or with their own struggles at home or school or personal lives . . . it was special.

—Kerrin Lyons, former TUFF Girls Assistant Director

Practicing Being a Protector in TUFF Girls: Becoming Protectors and Not Oppressors

Luzsil came to TUFF Girls when she was eleven. She loved doing yoga and getting to know everyone in the group by playing icebreaker games. She quickly got along with the other TUFF Girls, some who had been there for a while and some who were new. There was a lot going on at her home, which was true for most folks in TUFF Girls, and the space we co-created put her at ease. Luzsil's **gender expression** was more masculine, like her two older sisters.

During one of our overnights, I saw that Luzsil seemed a little down. I checked in but she said nothing was wrong. Candice pulled me aside and confessed that Mytrice had told Luzsil she was in the wrong bathroom and that she should get dressed in the boys' bathroom. Candice said she spoke up and told Mytrice that was wrong of her to say, but Mytrice stuck to her comment. When I took Mytrice aside to ask if this was true, she said it was and that she didn't feel comfortable with Luzsil in the bathroom.

How do you think Luzsil felt about Mytrice's comment?

Why do you think Mytrice felt uncomfortable by Luzsil's presence?

What systems do you think were at play to make them feel the way they felt?

At that moment I didn't talk about systems. I talked about **boundaries**. I asked Mytrice if Luzsil had said or physically done anything to **harm** her in or outside of the bathroom. She said she hadn't. I asked her if Luzsil had shown her respect and kindness, and she said she had. I asked her how her words might have made Luzsil feel, and she seemed to soften. Just a little bit.

"It probably made her feel bad, but I don't agree with people being gay, it's against my religion."

I responded, "From what you shared with me Luzsil didn't cross any of your **boundaries**, she was merely existing. In this space, you don't get to cross her **boundaries** for existing. And I don't think your religion teaches you to disrespect people who are respectful and kind to you, does it?" She agreed it didn't and she agreed, on her own, to apologize to Luzsil for the comment.

The next week we talked about the system of **heterosexism** and how it privileges people who are straight. The teaching assistants and I also talked about **gender expression**, and how there are many ways a person can choose to express their **gender**. Mytrice and Luzsil were quiet in that conversation, but many of the other girls who remembered the incident spoke up and agreed: our job was to support people in what felt good and healthy in their bodies. This too was a part of turning up for freedom.

This **principle** of being a **protector** was about keeping each other safe in the face of a culture of **patriarchy** that defined **power** as conquering people. To be a **protector** said that stepping into leadership was about individual and collective survival. Candice exercised her **privilege** in that overnight by defending Luzsil, and we were all better for it.

Slow Down with Me

Slow down with me and consider all the ways those with privilege could do better and not be mean or rude:

- How might cis girls advocate that their schools allow for trans girls to use girls' bathrooms or a gender-neutral bathroom for nonbinary students?
- How might students whose parents have economic privilege not flash their new clothes or phones in front of friends and peers who don't?

- How might light-skinned girls refuse to laugh at or make jokes made about dark-skinned girls in social media comments or during a fight?
- How might girls who live with their families refuse to feed the rumor mill about girls in foster care or who don't have a secure place to live?

Figure 2.1: Candice, Anjelica, Luzsil, Nyjah, and Jazcitty moderating and presenting a panel on safe spaces at 2016 Black Girl Project Conference.

TUFF Girls tried to practice this **principle** of **protection** by creating intentional spaces to hold space for us to process and channel our collective pain into collective **power**. In our weekly circles we were processing fights at school. We were celebrating the hair and bodies that mainstream media has taught us to judge and punish. We were questioning why their schools had less **resources** than schools attended by mostly white children. We were having deep conversations about what it would take for young people to unite and create more safety and **justice** where they live and go to school. Deep as those conversations got, as you read earlier, sometimes TUFF Girls still made it tough for other TUFF Girls.

This chapter is going to ask you to take care of yourself as you read it because we are talking about safety and the experience of not feeling safe. That can make you feel anxious and even hopeless. Continue to check in with your body and ask yourself what it needs to feel present. Remember the tools from Chapter 1, remember your breath, and remember to take your time. Practicing the **principle** of being a **healer** was about paying attention to what you were feeling inside and being intentional with how you responded to what you noticed.

Let's Get Into It: Patriarchy 101

So how did we get to this place where Black and Brown children have become so unprotected? For starters, the history of European **colonization** and slavery in the United States and in the world forced people of African descent to accept and assimilate to the harmful beliefs of **patriarchy**. The matriarchies, or women-centered networks of **power**, that existed in Africa before **colonization** not only practiced passing leadership positions down through the women of the family, but also saw equality between many **genders**.

Over centuries, however, **patriarchy** has created a culture and mindset that **privileges** cis boys/men and masculinity by defining them as more rational, more intelligent, and natural leaders and protectors. **Patriarchy demands** that boys and men be more sexual (towards people who express femininity) and aggressive (towards everyone) in order to demonstrate being "strong" or "real." In **patriarchy, femmes** and **trans** people are the "weaker **sex**." It dismisses our feelings, experience, and even our humanity. Today we see this in our music, in our media, and even in how we handle each other on the street and in the home. **Femmes** and **gender-expansive** folks are punished for being strong or simply existing since they are seen as objects to be controlled by boys and men to be at their service.

Youth in TUFF Girls could easily name the ways they experienced or witnessed violence of **patriarchy**. Perhaps the hardest kind of violence to discuss was sexual **harm** since we often don't talk about that in our families or even in our schools. **Rape culture** includes how acts of sexual **harm** are seen as normal. The history of slavery impacts how Black girls are sexualized by adults and why **rape culture** impacts them at higher rates. Indigenous girls also experience higher rates of sexual assault. Indigenous scholars and **activists** say that the history of settler colonialism has sparked cycles of **trauma** that led to this harsh reality.

In Chapter 1, I mentioned that one in four Black girls will experience sexual assault by the time she reaches eighteen. Probably like many of you reading this, I am one of those statistics. Unfortunately, I was sexually violated many times in my childhood, in the very spaces that were supposed to keep me safe. In each incident, the violation was either done by an adult, witnessed by an adult, or occurred with adults nearby.

> *Breathe with me. If you have water nearby, take a few sips, nice and slow. If you don't, pause your reading until you can find some.*

At six years old, a lunch mother who was supposed to supervise us children during recess watched as two boys pinned me down and lifted up my school uniform. They stood over me and stared at my panties. The lunch mother said nothing when we locked eyes while I was lying on the ground. I was scared and embarrassed, and was silent afterwards, just like that lunch mother.

If that sparks a memory, rub your hands together until they are warm. Place them over your heart. Now over your belly. Feel the warmth of your energy.

In order to get to my high school freshman year from the Bronx to the Lower East Side of Manhattan, I had to take two trains and a bus. On the very first day of school, the 5 train was so packed with people, we were shoulder to shoulder. In my headphones was Eve, the rapper from Philly who had just dropped her first album. I thought the man behind me kept bumping into me because of how the train was moving from side to side. I kept inching forward, but I kept feeling him and a fast motion which was too close for comfort. I blocked out the disgusting feeling that he was relieving himself on me. He wouldn't dare do something like that so publicly, I told myself. But when I finally got off at 14th Street I turned around and saw him smile. I was fourteen and tucked that memory away for over a decade.

If that makes you feel tight in your body, bring your shoulders up by your ears as you take a deep inhale. Let out a growl as you exhale out.

At fifteen, I was watching a turkey bake in the oven for Thanksgiving when my aunt's husband grabbed me from behind with a half erection, pressing himself into my back for what felt like eternity. It was likely thirty seconds. My aunt, my mother, and my cousins were all upstairs as I stood there, paralyzed by shock. He let me go once he heard their footsteps coming back downstairs. The shame of feeling unable to protect myself once again helped me to stuff that memory in a dark closet inside myself. For years.

> *If that takes you to a familiar place or touches on some old pain, I want to remind you that it was not your fault. Wrap your arms around yourself and squeeze tight. Feel your feet on the floor. Your hips in your seat. Appreciate the breath and how it helps you stay connected to your body and to your* **power**. *Right here. Right now.*

Figure 2.2: Nyjah reading her speech at the 2015 March to End **Rape Culture**.

Healing for me did not begin until my early twenties, when I began to reflect on my childhood. Pain and anger in my belly motivated me to start therapy and talk to my family. This showed me that men are not the only protectors of **patriarchy**. Women do this work too. Years after the incident in the kitchen with my aunt's husband, I was finally able to tell my family what happened and had developed the courage to set a boundary: I would not be attending any family functions where he was present. He lied about his inappropriateness, telling my aunt and others that he was merely being affectionate. This suggested that I was overreacting. My aunt believed him and said she would not forgive me for "bringing pain to her family" by sharing my experience with others and asking for people to honor my boundary. Some family members believed me; many others chose not to get involved. It felt like they were wishing I would brush this under the rug like generations before me had done.

Some of you may read these stories of **harm** in my childhood and assume that I was a soft kid who let those things happen. While all violence is a shock to the system, sexual **harm** can lead to a deeper sense of feeling paralyzed, especially for children. Most importantly, children shouldn't have to be that tough. I share so that we can start focusing our attention on the adults engaging in disgusting behavior or adults expecting young Black kids to protect themselves without help.

If **patriarchy** encourages us to believe that men and our relationships with them have more value, then remaining blindly loyal or passive to men will always be easier than holding them accountable when they cause **harm**. This is why so many families experience cycles of **trauma** over generations. It is also why it is easier for many music fans to see R. Kelly as "innocent" and the girls he violated as simply "fast" and "ignorant." It is why so many people of different ages see Bill Cosby as innocent of drugging women and assaulting them since they believe those women were probably looking for fame anyway. These men and the people closest to them that supported their actions, need **healing** and **accountability** in order to shift the culture. This is true for anyone who commits sexual

harm and other forms of **harm** as well. Pretending to believe in their innocence or simply locking them away forever won't help them access that. Only dismantling the **patriarchy** in our culture will do that.

How do we all do the work of keeping each other safe?

It requires compassion and truth telling and trusting people to understand and love the bodies they are in. **Patriarchy** fails to do all of these things. In fact, **patriarchy** is a failure of true leadership, and it keeps us from getting free.

This principle of being a **protector** shakes up the idea that men are the natural protectors. Adults of all **genders** should be responsible enough to protect you from **harm**. And as young adults, more safety and **protection** are possible when we all make the brave choice to unlearn the toxic messages of **patriarchy** and do the work to keep each other safe.

Questions to Help You Spot a Trustworthy Adult

1. When you close your eyes and think of them, does your body relax or tighten up? Our gut will usually be our body's first signal to who or what feels safe.
2. Are they able to listen to you without interrupting? Are they able to give you full attention when you are telling them you have something important you want to share?
3. Are they able to apologize when making a mistake?
4. Do they listen to you when you tell them to stop hugging you/not to touch you or ask for consent when they hug you?
5. Do they believe you when you are telling the truth?

6. Do they take action when another person is harming you or if you are harming yourself?
7. Do you feel judged after you have told them about harm that has happened?

Practicing Being a Protector in TUFF Girls: Growing through Conflict

I was both excited and quietly worried when Brianna and Nyjah wanted to become part of the first cycle of TUFF Girls. They lived across the street from the community center in Hunting Park, just two houses down from each other, and went to the same school. When their friendship was strong, everyone around them became contagious with their humor and playfulness. But when the friendship was challenged by miscommunication, or tension between other friendship circles, things could get really tense and even mean. Several days before our first day of TUFF Girls, Brianna and Nyjah's conflict became physical. While they both agreed they wouldn't fight in the program, their pain and anger were felt in the room and in their side comments.

About two weeks into the program, it was brought to my attention that they were preparing to fight after school and before the program. That night I called their guardians and shared this information and asked if I could pick them up after school and take them on a hike for **healing**. Their folks agreed, and the next day at 3:09 p.m. I was parked in front of Bethune Elementary School with Welch's Fruit Snacks in the passenger seat. Nyjah groaned about having to do anything with Brianna, and Brianna refused to get in the car until I shared that I had those fruit snacks.

Once in the car I explained that it hurt me to see a friendship like theirs become violent. TUFF Girls was trying to create a space for girls to be honest and vulnerable, and work out tough issues like the ones they were having.

The weather felt a little bit like the energy in the car: cloudy, chilly, and sharp. Once we got to the Wissahickon Trail in Germantown, I shared that the only way for us to get warm was to walk. So we did, for almost a quarter mile. We eventually arrived at a section with hundreds of tiny rocks. Once there I shared that each of them had told me of insults or silent treatments they had experienced over the summer, and I wanted to give them an opportunity to name it, and let it go if they felt ready. I had them each pick up a rock that represented each time they felt disrespected over the summer. Hesitant and deeply annoyed at first, they eventually gathered about four to five rocks each. I asked them to give me their rocks, and then returned each girl's rocks to the other girl.

"We are going to keep hiking, and I want you to keep in mind, you are holding each other's pain. I want you to keep in mind that the reason you became such good friends is because of your ability to do just that—hold each other's pain."

I could feel the energy shift when I said this. Anger was cooling off into sadness. I had us walk down a stony hill that led to a running creek.

"Creeks and rivers are kind of like our emotions—they are made to flow. I think it's a part of why they are so peaceful to watch. They remind us of the harmony we want to feel inside. You can sit here and watch the creek flow. I invite you to also think about the pain you are holding in your hand. What does it mean to recognize that you caused pain even as you experienced it? What does 'letting it go' mean for you? That can't be forced, neither can forgiveness. But

I want to invite you to consider what you feel ready to forgive and say what you are forgiving the other person for out loud as you toss each rock."

It was a long three minutes of quiet before Nyjah stood up. I could sense that tucked under her tough exterior in that moment was a willingness to be vulnerable: to feel deeply for another person who had also caused her **harm**.

"I guess I'll start, or whatever. I say it to her?"

"Ideally, yes. But only if you are ready."

"Well, I guess, I forgive you for talking about me behind my back because I know I talked about you."

Brianna sat in agitation for a long time as Nyjah looked on in the river with anxious anticipation. We looked at the ripples of the creek for a long moment before Brianna finally looked at me and asked, "Is it my turn?"

"Only if you are ready."

"Well, Nyjah, I forgive you for calling me the 'b word,' and calling me out of my name. I know I called you a couple things."

With each rock thrown into the creek, the tension between the two friends loosened up and floated away, much like a dandelion in the wind. Emotions, once bottled up, flowed like the creek in front of us. Once there were no more rocks in their hands, they asked if they could collect more. Would you believe they took their forgiveness all the way back to second grade!

Growing through conflict often requires us to be creative in order to help people feel safe enough to work through the big and small feelings that come up when addressing **harm**. In this case, fruit snacks helped with after-school munchies, and the natural environment brought its own calm and centering presence.

After the hike, their relationship did not return back to normal and they didn't really speak much to each other after that. However, the relationship did *transform.* The **boundaries** between them were much clearer as they recommitted to mutual respect and empathy. They were accountable for the pain they had caused each other and agreed that they wanted peace between them. And all of us at TUFF Girls were made better for it.

I have heard many young people say they have no hope in their generation because of all the senseless violence they see in their lives and on social media. In these moments I try to pass down wisdom given to me by Black, Brown, Indigenous, and Asian elders: our imagination is one of the most powerful things we have for our survival. Liberating the mind from accepting **oppression** as normal is the first step towards any change in the future. When we commit to protecting our hope for the future, we are better able to see our small but necessary role for creating change and possibility within us and around us, right here and right now. We are able to start to believe the freedom fighter, Assata Shakur, when she says *we have nothing to lose but our chains.*

Let's Get Into It: Conflict, Justice, and the School-to-Prison Pipeline

Often, we are taught to see conflict as bad and to avoid it at all costs. But conflict is bound to happen in all relationship building. It is a healthy part of growing authentic and deeper relationships. How we handle it says a lot about our ability to practice repair and stay in connection with ourselves and each other. Unnecessary conflict—such as bullying or harassment—only helps to feed **systems of oppression** that keep us unfree. When we remember that protecting each other is a part of leadership, then we are better able to grow the muscle we need to handle conflict in productive ways.

Doing that work can be really hard though, especially when someone has been straight-up disrespectful. Or, in other cases, not honest about their intentions or actions. What do you do when someone has talked about you behind your back and refuses to admit it when you confront them? What happens if they are your friend? Or a family member? What are the options that are available to you that allow you to be truthful without also being harmful?

Today, there is a whole **movement** of people who are maintaining the lessons of Indigenous **ancestors** such

Restorative justice (RJ) is this belief that we can address conflict and violence in ways that center **healing** and **accountability** without causing more **harm**.

Transformative justice (TJ) is this belief that in order to do **restorative justice** we have to change the political and social conditions that encouraged us to cause **harm** in the first place.[1]

---

[1] We won't discuss transformative justice (TJ) in depth in this book since this is a lot more advanced than restorative justice, and potentially more difficult for young people to facilitate. However, there are books about it at the end of this chapter which offer lots of stories about what this could look like. The source I cite here for the definition of transformative justice is a great resource: see Sara Kershnar, Staci Haines, Gillian Harkins, Alan Greig, Generation Five, "Towards Transformative Justice Guide: A Liberatory Approach to Child Sexual Abuse & Other Forms of Intimate & Community Violence," June 2007, https://criticalresistance.org/wp-content/uploads/2020/05/G5_Toward_Transformative_Justice-Document.pdf.

as the Navajo Nation,[1] who sought to allow conflict to strengthen the community through dialogue and ritual. Much of these practices are where **restorative justice (RJ)** comes from. This wisdom has also been kept alive for centuries by people who don't believe that police, prisons, or the state can address the root causes of conflict, **harm**, and **abuse**. In fact, these people believe that the **oppression** of the state has created the conditions for a lot of the violence we encounter.

When an individual is committing to **restorative justice** it is because they don't want to participate in cycles of disrespect, violence, or **trauma**. Instead, they want to create a space for a process of **healing** where their humanity is also respected and recognized. Creating the conditions for each person to see each other honestly not only takes a lot of courage and integrity, but often requires the support of other people to help hold the space and a belief that **healing** and personal transformation is possible. When it comes to **accountability**, we all can benefit from trusted guidance to do the personal work of taking responsibility and changing our thoughts and behavior.

There are some schools in the US that have committed to **restorative justice** by scheduling time for relationship building between students, and between students and teachers. The idea is that people are more likely to be accountable to keeping a community safe if they also feel like they belong and are valued in that community. This might look like having a regular "circle practice." Different circles have different purposes. Circle practices, like "**healing** circles," come to us from Indigenous communities. These communities often

---

[1] Laura Mirsky, "Restorative Justice Practices of Native American, First Nation and Other Indigenous People of North America: Part One," Restorative Practices e-Forum (2004), https://www.iirp.edu/images/pdf/natjust1.pdf.

use a Talking Stick to facilitate sharing or speaking within a group. This is usually a special wooden stick held only by the person talking at the time. They pass this around as they collectively work through tensions or important decisions.

Circle practices help a group of people create the culture of a space, whereby that culture is strong enough to offer **healing** and **accountability** when people of the group need it. A "daily morning circle" will allow a person to check in on how they feel, while also sharing thought-provoking questions that help people bond and strengthen each other. A sample question is: *What growth in yourself are you proud of?* A "peace circle" may be called when there is a conflict between two people or as a way to address a **harm** that has been caused.

Below I will share tips on how to use **restorative justice** with your crew, at your school, and in your community.

Restorative Justice *with Your Crew*

Chances are you have probably already tried to do some **restorative justice** work with your friends. Your friend might have said or done something to you, and you decided to fight for the friendship by pulling them aside and sharing how you felt their actions impacted you. They may have heard you out, made it smaller than what it was, or been in complete denial. It may have been smaller than what it was or you might have been completely on point. In return, your friendship might have gotten stronger, stayed the same, gone into a weird limbo place, or it might have ended all together.

The truth is, a part of getting older and discovering your **power** is also getting clearer on your **boundaries** and what you are willing to accept from a friend, and how you want to grow with people. **Boundaries** are an invisible line that you don't want someone to cross. **Restorative justice** is not about expecting you to be friends with everyone or return things back to a "normal." Rather, it is saying that no matter what happens, I am willing to see the other person as a human who makes mistakes and is worthy of dignity, just like me. Most of us are trying to do the best we can with what we have. We are all working through different **traumas** and **systems of oppression** that will impact all of our relationships; especially the ones closest to us. The problem is, many of us also aren't given the tools to try and work through conflict without getting distant or aggressive. Tough conversations are just that—tough. But what is made possible when we create a goal before we enter them?

Many **Indigenous people** used the ideas behind **restorative justice** in their educational practices before the Europeans came and **colonized** this land. Perhaps the most documented tribe is the Navajo Nation, which still exists. During the late 1800s and early 1900s, however, settlers required Indigenous children to attend "Indian boarding schools" scattered throughout the nation. Teachers and school administrators did not allow the Indigenous students to practice their culture, speak their language, or be in contact with their families. Youth who refused these rules were beaten, and in some cases, killed or left to die.[1] Robert H. Pratt, the US Army officer who opened the Carlisle Boarding School in Carlisle, Pennsylvania had a motto: "Kill the Indian, save the man." These schools were eventually shut down due

[1] Roxanne Dunbar-Ortiz, *An Indigenous Peoples' History of the United States for Young People* (Boston: Beacon Press, 2019), 163–165.

to Indigenous resistance and organizing. Today, that organizing continues to get more **resources** redistributed to reservations and protects sacred lands from the financial interests of large corporations.

Restorative Justice *at Your School*

In the late 1990s, a tragedy occurred that completely shifted how schools dealt with safety. On April 20, 1999, two young white men killed thirteen of their classmates in this country's first mass school shooting. This tragedy rocked more than just the small town of Columbine, Colorado where it happened, but the entire United States. This act of violence happened in a suburban high school with mostly white students. The event encouraged states across the nation to invest money in metal detectors and school resource officers (SROs), also known as "school police." From 1997 to 2007, the number of SROs increased by one third and Black students were three times more likely to be suspended than white students.[2] School police are not trained in responding to behaviors characteristic of young people experiencing the hormonal changes of adolescence, let alone Black and Brown girl-identified youth experiencing **trauma**.[3] This meant that they were treated like mini-adult criminals. If money in already struggling urban schools was being spent on creating police stations in schools, how much

---

[2] Jonathan Stith, "#ENDWARONYOUTH: Building a Youth Movement for Black Lives and Educational Justice," *Lift Us Up, Don't Push Us Out!: Voices from the Front Lines of the Educational Justice Movement*, ed. Mark Warren (Boston: Beacon Press, 2018), 83.

[3] Monique Morris, *Pushout: The Criminalization of Black Girls in Schools* (New York: The New Press, 2016).

money was being spent on educational **resources** like counselors, science labs, and technology? It makes me think about what **scholar-activist** Angela Davis said about schools:

> When children attend **schools** that place a greater value on discipline and security than on knowledge and intellectual development, they are attending prep schools for prison. Justice is indivisible. You can't decide who gets civil rights and who doesn't.[4]

In many ways, Davis is describing the **school-to-prison pipeline**. This is the process of targeting Black and Brown students by criminalizing their behaviors and pushing them to enter the criminal **justice** system at an earlier age than their white counterparts. **Patriarchy** and its policing of **gender** also impacts girl-identified youth differently. For example, according to 2018 data from the US Department of Education Office for Civil Rights, Black girls are six times more likely to be expelled, three times more likely to be suspended, and four times more likely to be arrested than white girls. "School pushout" is a punitive practice that excludes students from the classroom or school, disproportionately affects Black and Brown students, and leads to learning loss and ultimately to incarceration.

For over twenty years, **organizers** for education **justice** have developed local and state **campaigns** that challenged the various ways the **school-to-prison pipeline** was targeting Black and Brown students. They made **demands** for smaller class sizes, more teachers of color, updated technology, more counselors, the removal of metal detectors and of school

---

[4] Angela Davis, *Are Prisons Obsolete?* (New York: Seven Stories Press, 2003), 38–39.

police, and more support for **restorative justice** when addressing issues of conflict, **harm**, and violations. In 2014, the US government shared new guidelines for all schools, recommending that schools use restorative practices to build positive school climates. While this recognition from the government showed that creating a police state in schools does not create a safe learning environment, the struggle for all schools to have all of what they need for **restorative justice** and be a place of safety continues until this day.

If your school has not discussed restorative practices or doesn't have any policies or practices around it, you and the adults in your life should consider organizing with other students and families to **demand** that it does. School districts in Chicago, IL and Oakland, CA have **restorative justice** policies that were earned through students, teachers, and families organizing together. Fighting for **restorative justice** to happen at your school requires that the administration and staff are all trained in restorative and **trauma**-informed practices, and they make this training available to parents and students as well. It also means updating their school policies on conduct in their handbooks.

Schools that are truly committed to **restorative justice** should be doing a lot of community building and providing support. This could look and feel like the following:

- Circle practices, where you build deeper relationships with your peers and your teachers.
- Social-emotional learning activities that help young people and adults practice empathy, compassion, trust building, and deep reflection on **trauma** and resiliency.
- Political education about the history of **systems of oppression**, **anti-Blackness**, **gender** and sexual identities, **consent**, as well as conversations about

poverty that are humanizing for people without access to **resources**.

- When you have disobeyed the rules or caused **harm**, circles or parent-teacher conferences are held in which you are asked to explain the reason behind your actions and expected to *make it right*. Making it right might look like making a commitment to changed behavior, or community service that relates to the behavior, or both.

- Helping you understand that when someone holds us accountable, you may feel this as discomfort, but you should also feel supported in the idea that you can grow and change from that mistake.

- If **restorative justice** is being used by school staff to address a physical fight or conflict between students, each person needs to be coached before going into a mediation. The following questions also need to be asked: *Are you ready? What is the goal? What ground rules are important to lay down so that you feel ready to be vulnerable and accountable?* The goal is not to apologize and apologies should never be forced. The goal is to create a safe and respectful space to talk through the root cause of the issue. The goal might also be to create the **boundaries** necessary for dealing with each other in the future, especially if you aren't able to see each other's position after having had a dialogue. Students should be doing more talking than the teacher themselves.

- If **restorative justice** is being used between a student and a teacher, then ideally a parent or another adult supporter, like a counselor, is present. Students should have the space to name the impact. Teachers should be modeling honesty and vulnerability and be willing to make things right if they have caused **harm**.

Figure 2.3: Restoring our traditions for transforming **harm**. Illustration by Pascale Ife Williams (2023).

Restorative Justice *around the Way*

When someone jumps or assaults your sister or your friend on your block, chances are your instincts will tell you to either get them jumped or call the police. Retaliating starts a cycle of violence that could lead to damage that can't be undone or even death. There are some who would say that calling the police is the "right way" and the safest way to stop the violence. But we know that is not always a guarantee, especially for Black and Brown people or people with disabilities or mental illness. In some cases, situations have been escalated or not been handled well by the police, leading to damage that can't be undone and even death. Are there other ways to find **justice** and feel safe that don't involve engaging in more violence or relying on police?

I'm not going to lie. Trying to restore **harm** when it happens around the neighborhood can be a difficult and even impossible process, especially if it occurs between two people who don't know each other at all. Ideally, as we strengthen community around shared values, we could do the trust building needed to create teams of people to support the person who has been harmed, AND a team of people to support the person who caused **harm**. One team would listen to what the person harmed needs in order for **harm** to be addressed and for **healing** to occur, and both teams could support a process of **healing**, education, and a new set of healthy **boundaries** and conditions for that relationship.

So, the question we should ask ourselves is: **what do we need to create or strengthen in our neighborhoods in order to have the support required for healing and accountability for everyone?** This is why it's so important that people organize for better housing and work conditions, and for food security. People need their basic needs met. Without this, it is hard for **healing** to take place or to prevent community violence from happening.

When the Police Don't Come, Who Keeps Our Students Safe?: A Bonus Story[1]

For three years I worked at an alternative high school where many students enrolled after being pushed out from other schools for fighting. At El Centro de Estudiantes High School, there were no metal detectors, no school police, and very few fights. I attribute this to the fact that our principal led with his heart. We were a small school focused on relationship building, and we had three school counselors in the building committed to restorative justice. That intention and level of support is a reality all our students should have. However, once we changed principals and buildings and experienced budget cuts, our internal support system was compromised and violence increased. At the end of one of our school days this past fall, I could sense that a fight was about to break out. I kept asking the young women wrapping up their hair what was going on, but they ignored me, too focused on fear and survival. I heard one of them say, "They brought other men with them." I quickly sent a mass text to all the teachers and staff in the building to meet me outside for support, as I walked out of the building with the group of girls. Sure enough, there was a small group of young men in their twenties who were clearly agitated. One of them had his hand on his hip, as if to signal he had a gun.

[1] This story is from a speech I delivered in June 2020, at a rally organized by the Philadelphia Student Union for their Police-Free Schools campaign.

Against my instincts, but out of legal obligation, I called the dispatcher for school police who then called the Philadelphia Police Department since a possible gun was involved. By the time I finished the call, the group of girls and young men were arguing. As I wiggled my way in between the two groups, a dozen of our teachers, counselors, and staff ran over and together we eventually formed a line between our students and the young men. Nothing but threats were being exchanged, so we still had no clue about the relationship between our students and the young men, or what the conflict was about.

One of the men, who was the loudest of them all, was specifically pointing at and threatening Mi, one of our **trans** students. Knowing the kind of fatal violence that **transphobia** provokes, I stood in front of him. I kept my eyes on him and his fear and I kept asking him in a very even tone: "What happened, I want to hear your side, let me hear you out. I see an adult threatening a child and I don't want anyone to get hurt." I repeated this until he finally said, "You wouldn't understand. It started two years ago." An opening.

So, I pushed, "What happened two years ago?" He ignored me at first, but I kept repeating, "What happened? I see men threatening girls right now and I need you to help me keep us all safe." After a few minutes of this, he eventually started to talk to me. He told me how the fight started between their family members. How just two weeks ago there was a rumble that he and Mi got pulled into. As he began to share, the other young men with him gathered around him, and our staff was able to bring our students further away. Retelling the events while still hearing threats from other students meant he was still very angry and yelling threats. I was firm in saying, "I couldn't allow that kind of violence to happen to my students." At one point, another young man told me, "I'm from the

Bronx, you wouldn't understand," and I said, "Baby, I'm from the Bronx too. I understand that the Bronx is just like Philly. That we are hurting, and we are afraid, and we need change. These cycles of **harm** are getting us nowhere."

The line of teachers and counselors were able to walk our students back to the building to listen to their side of the story. One other teacher stood with me in the rain for nearly thirty minutes as we listened to these young men continue to release anger, and eventually, fears of a pregnant girlfriend getting caught up in the beef and losing the child. I shared that I didn't know them but that I cared about them AND our students. That my heart broke to see us hurt each other and repeat the violence that kills us or feeds our prison system. I mentioned the police were on the way, but I didn't think they would keep us safe. I said, "Conversations like this keep us safe." They were not ready to mediate, but they felt heard by myself and my fellow teacher, Mr. O. They were receptive to our genuine gestures of care. They made verbal commitments to not show up to the school with arms, or to fight, and to call me if there was more conflict. And then, literally as we shook hands, one cop car lazily pulled up next to us. I told the officers we were fine, and sure enough, the young men did not return to the school for the remainder of the year.

The important takeaway here is the fact that the police did not keep us safe that day, even when we called them for help. What kept us safe was our collective courage, collective action, and collective care. We don't need police; we need *us*. So please repeat after me: poor students, **trans** students, Black students, all students ARE people, and all people deserve to feel safe, to feel seen, to feel like they belong, and to feel like they have the capacity to grow, and that the people around them believe that too.

Tools for Practicing Being a Protector

This section will offer some questions and ideas to consider practicing to become a **protector**; such as, by de-escalating conflict where you can and tending to the heart and body when conflict has turned physical.

Table 2.1: Things to consider when trying to work through conflict.

Questions to Ask Yourself	Ideas to Consider
What was the true impact of that person's action on my heart? Underneath my anger and pride, is there sadness that they betrayed my trust? How can I take care of myself emotionally?	Anger is a natural emotion to an injustice, and often that is what betrayal feels like. This is why the first principle is to be a **healer of self** so that you can use those **healing** tools to be resilient by processing anger in healthy ways. That way, your anger does not master you and your relationships.
What do I want from the other person? Is it an apology or is it changed behavior? Both? Or is it some act of service and a commitment to do better?	It can be helpful to do some writing around these questions or talk to a trustworthy and responsible friend/adult. This will help you to process your anger, and also, to create a vision in your mind for how you want them to make it right.
What is the best environment to do this in, for a conversation to be honest, vulnerable, and real? What do you need to do to feel ready? Have you thought about whether that other person is ready to have this conversation?	In my experience, these kinds of conversations rarely go well if there is no careful preparation in handling it as a sensitive conversation. For example, these are not conversations that go well on social media, or through text messaging, or when you don't have a lot of time, or in large open spaces like hallways or auditoriums. People need to feel safe, in order to trust that the information that is being presented is coming from a good place.

Should this be a one-on-one conversation? Is there another peer or adult that we both trust to support us?	A lot can be done in one-on-one (1:1) conversations with the other person when we practice courage in being honest and fair. Some situations can be resolved with other mature and trustworthy people in the space, especially if it feels like 1:1 conversation isn't helpful anymore. I encourage you to reflect on what you feel and ask yourself: are you ready and able; what do you hope to gain from the conversation; and, what kind of relationship do you have with the other person?

So You Fought. Now What? Tools to Use before and after a Fight

It may feel unrealistic to expect young people to simply not fight when protecting each other or themselves, especially if someone hits you first and/or you feel like you are being attacked. **Effective communication** can usually help reduce the chances of a physical altercation, but achieving that can be extremely difficult, especially when people see fighting as a demonstration of strength and/or feel extremely threatened.

Bodies hold onto traumatic experiences, so if you have ever experienced a bad fight or been physically attacked, we may make decisions on the need to protect ourselves from experiencing that again. Some folks call it "blacking out" or "seeing red." Chemicals in our brain designed for our survival are being released, sometimes, causing us to have a response that does not match the level of threat in front of us. Or, to actually match the level of threat in front of us.

Here are some things to do and think about if you get pushed to that point:

- Breathe deeply and squeeze your hands in open and closed fists so that you can be as calm and clear in responding to the threat. Who or what can help keep you safe?

- Slow down and take time to heal if you did in fact fight. When your body perceives a huge threat, chemicals called endorphins will be released in order to give you the energy to fight or flight and survive. It takes a while for those endorphins to wear off, so you might not feel the pain or sore-ness of having been hit for several hours or even days. Your brain is also not thinking clearly. Soak in a tub of Epsom salt to help ease pain and reduce swelling of where you were hit. You can find Epsom salt at the dollar store or your local supermarket/pharmacy.

- Check in with your **ego**. In some cases, the fight might be the end of the beef. In other cases, the fight might have escalated it to another level. Usually, the person who felt like they lost or got sucker punched/jumped will feel the need to retali-ate and prove themselves. For the health and safety of you and our community I ask you to consider the following questions:

  - ❤ What is it that you actually need? Underneath the feelings for revenge, is it the need to be safe, respected, and treated with dignity? Are there more creative ways you can get those needs met that don't cause more **harm**? Who else can help you answer that question?

  - ❤ Who or what is at risk if you continue a cycle of violence? Who else can help you interrupt that cycle and be firm in your boundary?

  - ❤ What is the pain of this conflict teaching you about yourself and your relationships to other people?

Mistakes as Medicine

A part of what made this principle challenging to practice in TUFF Girls is because of how the **systems of oppression** are violence to our bodies. They set everyone up to judge one another. Additionally, since people in **power** are not made accountable when they cause **harm**, we easily confuse this for real **power**. This is why so many people don't want to be free, they simply want to be the oppressor.

This is also why political education is so important, and why our next principle involves being a **scholar-activist**. If you are unaware that we live in a capitalist society that teaches us that people with more money have a right to judge, then you model this. If you did not learn from school or at home that before **colonization**, there were African cultures that had many **genders** not just two, or that there were same-**gender** love relationships, then you will judge **trans** girls or queer folks. You may believe that this is something only white people do. If you believe that reading books is "acting white," then you will judge Black and Brown people who do.

But leadership for Black and Brown girls, stepping into our **power**, is not about stepping into the shoes of our oppressors. Nah. To be oppressive may seem like you are free to **abuse** others and therefore powerful, but you are losing your humanity in the process. Our **ancestors** and our descendants are asking for us to think about **power** in a deeper way. They are asking for us to not feed **systems of oppression** with our minds and bodies. They are asking us to think about a leadership that strives to free ourselves from the mental chains of superiority and hate. In order for us to do this and to know peace, then we are also asked to **study** war.

Questions for Reflection:

1. When are moments where you felt protected by someone else? When have you protected someone else? How did you feel in each of those instances?
2. How did reading the stories in this chapter make you think about your own experiences with conflict?
3. How do you typically handle conflict? Do you avoid it, become petty, take it head on, or something else? Where do you think there is room for growth and maturity?

Recommended Reading:

Feminist AF: A Guide to Crushing Girlhood, Brittney Cooper, Chanel Craft Tanner, and Susana Morris
Educational Resources, Project NIA, https://project-nia.org/educational-resources
Something is Wrong: Exploring the Roots of Youth Violence, ed. Mariame Kaba, J. Cyriac Mathew, and Nathan Haines
Fumbling Towards Repair: A Workbook for Community Accountability Facilitators, Mariame Kaba and Shira Hissan
Beyond Survival: Stories and Strategies of the Transformative Justice Movement, ed. Ejeris Dixon and Leah Lakshmi Piepzna-Samarasinha
The Little Book of Restorative Justice, Howard Zehr
Sister Outsider, Audre Lorde
A Teen's Guide to the 5 Love Languages: How to Understand Yourself and Improve All Your Relationships, Dr. Gary Chapman

Playlist for Protection:

"Lean on Me," Bill Withers
"Count on Me," CeCe Winans and Whitney
    Houston
"What About Your Friends," TLC
"U.N.I.T.Y.," Queen Latifah
Rapsody, Eve (the whole album)
"Assata (Chant)," Sam Grant and April Goggans

CHAPTER 3

SCHOLAR-ACTIVIST

I like to think I know a lot, but I don't. I'm motivated to learn more.

—Yara Shahidi

TUFF Girls impacted me in a way in which I'm able to understand politics and participate in change actively. It helped me develop critical thinking skills and thinking for myself.

—Anjelica Love Speech, TUFF Girls Leader

My favorite part of TUFF Girls was the talks about our lives, the community, the government . . . talks that got real deep.

—Shari Cain, TUFF Girls Leader

Practicing Being a Scholar-Activist in TUFF Girls: Listening to Our People

In Fall 2015, TUFF Girls began the process of a participatory action research project (PAR). Much like the name suggests, PAR is a research project that invites the community to participate in order to investigate problems within it and create solutions towards action. This form of research felt like the perfect way to practice how we were thinking about **scholar-activism.** Kerrin and I had been inspired by the work of Girls of Gender Equity in Brooklyn, NY, where youth leaders had used the PAR model to look at how Black and Brown girls were singled out in unique ways by school resource officers (SROs). Whether it was being forced to remove bobby pins from their hair which set off a metal detector machine, or shamed for their voluptuous bodies by school administrators, they were punished in ways Kerrin and I had seen our TUFF Girls be punished. Our circle check-ins revealed this.

When we shared with the TUFF Girls our vision to use PAR to do a deeper dive into an area they felt passionate about, they were curious and eager. Together we decided to have a freedom party where we held a dinner and a focus group with some of their peers and family members to help us narrow down our focus. Over tacos and nachos in the warmth of my kitchen, the conversation kept coming back to harsh discipline at the elementary school they attended. At first, they were excited to have a clear focus and do more research. But they eventually saw that this asked for a lot of work and a lot of patience on their part.

It also asked for a lot of confidence from them to be able to have serious conversations with their peers about what was happening in school. We held another freedom party to collect stories and experiences from peers. This took place at the community center and allowed folks to write out their experiences on ribbons or share them on an open mic. We then marched to the school and tied the ribbons onto a fence that was famous for after-school fights. We wanted to let the school know the community knew what was happening. For Maniya Bey, TUFF Girls leader:

> I would say my favorite would be the time we led a march. It was dark but we walked all the way from the rec to my school, and when we went to

Figure 3.1: Focus dinner where we listened to youth outside of TUFF Girls, discussing the kinds of injustices they experienced at their schools.

my school, we tied ribbons on the gate. I'll forever cherish that moment because so many people in the community joined, and it actually felt like we were making a difference.

Figure 3.2: The families and peers of TUFF Girls hanging up their ribbons with their stories during our march to Bethune Elementary School. Maniya is pictured here at the bottom far right, next to her sister Brandy.

This was the first phase: naming the issue. The next phase was researching other attempts at our **campaign** so we could develop an action plan. But when we tried to move forward, TUFF Girls dug their heels in the ground. They were tired of the project and talking about the same thing. It felt boring and lacked any fun, they said. Kerrin and I were stumped. We wanted them to see it through, but we also wanted to respect and follow their leadership. So we did. We took a pause and never went back to the project.

Why else do you think they got tired of researching harsh discipline at school?
Is that a topic you would have wanted to focus on and create solutions around?

* * *

If you aren't making mistakes, however, it means you aren't trying. Here is what we learned from trying:

1. Doing research or exploration on a struggle that you are still living through is really hard. Super hard. At times I forgot how hard it was because I was not in their shoes. Making room for fun is super important. I think, at times, I put more pressure on TUFF Girls than was needed for a new **organization**. We all lost sight of our first principle to be a **healer of self**, and we paid the price.
2. Make collecting stories more fun by using art and/ or technology. Remind yourself and your crew that change takes time and consistency, and if we make it fun, we can have the stamina to be patient and consistent.
3. Make sure everyone feels excited or deeply curious about the issue. Talk about some potential barriers and how you might want to problem solve for them ahead of time.
4. Sometimes you start a project, and it doesn't work out the way you think it will and that's okay. We made the mistake of not going back to the PAR project altogether, since even the mention of the word PAR upset the girls. It's a fine line between too much pressure and pushing people out of their comfort zone. Walking that line is where change happens.

Ironically, almost five years after we ended the PAR project, Jazcitty Muniz, one of our TUFF Girls leaders, reflected in our sunsetting process that the PAR project was one of her favorite activities. I laughed when I heard this because she was the most vocal one about ending it! She didn't seem to remember this. In my gut, I knew that her initial experience of doing more reading and researching on a topic asked her to be patient in practicing different learning processes than the ones she was using at school. Often school treats knowledge and learning as very black and white: you are either right or wrong, slow or fast. It's easy to then internalize that and think of your intelligence in very black or white terms: either you are smart or not, and if you don't get the "answer" right away, then you are not. Yikes!

Let's go ahead and take a nice deep breath, dear one. Help the brain and the heart with an even deeper inhale this time, and a bigger exhale. Take your time. We can be so incredibly hard on ourselves, especially when thinking about our intelligence.

I know that was the case for me. In middle school, when I represented my sixth-grade class in the all-school spelling bee and then lost in the fourth round, Ms. Rivielo mocked me in front of all my peers as I walked back into the room. She didn't consider the pressure I felt as one of the few Black kids on that stage; how anxious I was displaying my intelligence in front of the whole school; or how embarrassed I felt as my white teacher then made fun of me for making a mistake in front of my whole class.

School should be a safe place for you to make mistakes, but when it isn't, it can keep you from wanting to try. Her insensitive response didn't keep me from trying, but it did encourage a lot of insecurities around my intelligence for a long time. That's because it wasn't just Ms. Rivielo that made me feel self-conscious.

Most of my middle and high school teachers—most of whom were white—gave little affirmation when I did get things right and expressed annoyance when I got things wrong.

Let's Get Into It: Thinking, Reading, and Writing for Freedom . . . Not Just to Be "Right"

According to INCITE! Women of Color Against Violence, PAR is "a way of collecting information for organizing that honors, centers, and reflects the experiences of people most directly affected by issues in our communities." The PAR project was our clearest example of **scholar-activism** in practice, but not the only one. In a more traditional sense, **scholar-activists** are "academics who are a bridge between the academy and the communities they serve."[1] "The academy" is another phrase for college or university. Although my training in research came from the academy, I don't believe young people need to wait for college or attend it to learn these tools or how to use these tools to address issues in their community. **Scholar-activism** inside TUFF Girls was not about getting things quickly or individually performing for a grade. It was about thinking, reading, and writing for the purpose of addressing injustice or inequality. It was about emotional and political freedom.

    Scholar-activism has looked like reading our stories through books and newspapers, but also doing deep listening when people describe their lived experiences. In fact, for most people of African and Indigenous

---

[1] Alvaro Huerta, "Viva the Scholar-Activist!" March 29, 2018, https://www.insidehighered.com/advice/2018/03/30/importance-being-scholar-activist-opinion.

descent, sharing stories by word of mouth, also known as "oral history," has been the main way that our cultural wisdom and practices have survived the violence of **colonization** and enslavement. Oral history can look like storytelling around the kitchen table. In a more formal way, it happens through individual interviews, or group interviews, also known as a focus group. That is what TUFF Girls did at our freedom party dinners to determine the focus of our PAR project.

Practicing **scholar-activism** as a **principle** of leadership looks like not only relying on school to teach us but also educating ourselves for ourselves and for our communities. It is reading, writing, and thinking about the past and/or current conditions of **oppression**, and using that reflection to transform yourself and your community. Studying the larger history of our communities can help us explain how and why we continue to live in a world of endless war where people in **power** disrespect our **power** and dignity.

Chances are you may have encountered a teacher or an auntie or afterschool program leader who was a **scholar-activist**. They were someone who might have sat you down and told you the history of the family and past stories of slavery or **racism**. They might have gone off their "teacher script" and spoken about Claudette Colvin, the fifteen-year-old Black girl who refused to give up her seat on the bus before Rosa Parks. Colvin did not make the history textbooks or mainstream media at the time because she was dark-skinned, pregnant, and unmarried. Those teachers or aunties may have shared examples like these to help question what you have been taught by the media, as well as at school. This kind of radical truth-telling is important for all leaders and these people are a gift. You should thank them if you have one in your life. If you don't, know that they exist.

There is an old saying that goes, "when the student is ready, the teacher will come."

This book is an example of **scholar-activism**. It attempts to bring research, history, and lived experience together for the purpose of leadership development of Black and Brown youth. If you have made it this far in the book, then you are on the path of becoming a **scholar-activist** if you aren't already. I love that for you.

School is usually the place where you are required to think, read, and write. And yet, depending on the school you attend and your learning style, that might be really hard to do. For example, it is difficult to want to learn in a place and with people who haven't affirmed you as an intelligent person or if you struggle with how people have tried to teach you things in school. Not all schools are like the ones that we see on television, especially if you are attending a school that does not have a lot of money and **resources**. Often these schools with fewer **resources** have very large classes, a lot of fights, little to no technology, more cops than counselors, and A LOT of worksheets.

Even if you do go to a school that is well resourced like a private school, these schools may practice **anti-Blackness** by forcing students to read the historical accomplishments of European people while leaving out the impact of their violence on communities of color. If we are not conscious of this, we can easily believe that what is right and beautiful comes from white people. This encourages us to become disconnected from our own history and have a one-sided perspective of our folks.

From this limited point of view, we can begin to judge ourselves and others who look like us since we are unaware of our own standards of intelligence and beauty. We may lash out and call each other what Europeans called us for centuries: "dumb," "lazy," and "ugly." This kind of name-calling was very common in slavery, and if we begin the history of Black people at slavery, or learn about African history from a European perspective, then we are likely to accept those stereotypes as true and repeat that name-calling.

But what if we knew about Queen Amina of Ancient Zaria, who was a great military strategist and professional soldier? Or Queen Rana Valona, who fought for Madagascar to be independent from European **powers** in the 1800s and even won an attack by the French on the coast of the country. What if Cleopatra, the famous North African queen whose clever mind and beauty won the respect and admiration of many rulers during her time, was not represented in Hollywood by white women, but the darker, honey-skin color that is much more common to people who live in that region of the world.

Once we take our education into our own hands, in order to understand who we are and learn the skills to achieve our goals, we no longer rely so heavily on school to determine intelligence, or to learn all that we need. We understand that the information we need is out there and we can find it on our own. That is exactly what **scholar-activists** have done throughout space and time. Explore all the different ways they have done this through their lived examples.

Tools for Practicing Scholar-Activism

There is an old racist saying that if you want to keep something from a Black person, then put it in a book. Wild, right? That kind of belief has led to the stereotype that Black people don't read. There are a few dangers to this: (1) it leaves out the history of there being a time when it was illegal for Black people to learn how to read or to teach others, which is why that saying even exists; (2) many of us were taught to

Examples of Scholar-Activists

Angela Davis

DOB: 1/26/1944
Zodiac sign: Aquarius
Place of birth: Birmingham, AL
Scholar-activism: Wrote several books, including, *Are Prisons Obsolete?* This helped to spark the imagination about a world beyond prisons and inspired a **movement** of people called "prison abolitionists."

Malala Yousafzai

DOB: 7/12/1997
Zodiac sign: Cancer
Place of birth: Mingora, Pakistan
Scholar-activism: After the Taliban made it illegal for girls to go to school in her town in Pakistan, Malala began speaking out against this publicly. She was targeted and eventually attacked by a gunman. She survived and became stronger and louder in her advocacy, earning her the Nobel Peace Prize in 2014.

Stella Nyanzi

DOB: 6/16/1974
Zodiac sign: Gemini
Place of birth: Masaka, Uganda
Scholar-activism: Poet, medical anthropologist, queer rights **activist** whose research has focused on **sexuality** and the **LGBTQIA** community. Has been arrested several times for her criticism of the Ugandan president, including a poem critiquing him and the first lady's refusal to distribute sanitary napkins to students in schools.

Janna Jihad

DOB: 4/6/2006

Zodiac sign: Aries

Place of birth: West Bank, Palestine

Scholar-activism: After two of her family members were killed by the Israeli army, Janna Jihad started to report on the military occupation of her Palestine hometown of Nabi Salih, from a youth's perspective. Originally using her mother's iPhone, she reported in Arabic and English and then would upload onto social media. In doing so, she earned more than 270,000 followers on Facebook.

Marley Dias

DOB: 1/3/2005

Zodiac sign: Capricorn

Place of birth: Philadelphia, PA

Scholar-activism: Disappointed by the amount of young adult (YA) books that lacked a Black female protagonist, sixteen-year-old Marley Dias started a literacy **campaign** to find 1,000 books that did. To date, she has collected 13,000, and started a national conversation about this issue. She is also the author of the book, *Marley Gets It Done: And So Can You!*

Mari Copeny

DOB: 7/7/2007

Zodiac sign: Cancer

Place of birth: Flint, MI

Scholar-activism: When the local government of Flint, Michigan switched the source of the city's water to cut costs, it led to high amounts of lead which contaminated the water, making it undrinkable. During the water crisis, thirteen-year-old Mari Copeny gained national attention by writing to then-President Obama about the suffering happening to her and her hometown. She used this spotlight to discuss environmental **racism** and start fundraising projects, one of which included creating water filters that allowed the water in Flint to become drinkable again.

read through stories that were not written for us or by us—for many people, that can turn them off from reading because it can be hard to relate or find meaning in a book; (3) a lot of history books, even when they *are* written by us, can feel boring or out of reach, especially if they use a lot of unfamiliar words.

New words can feel like a locked door. But if we are patient with ourselves, we can open those locked doors by *building our vocabulary*. It may mean, in the beginning, reading a book or an essay takes longer than expected. The world of understanding that can exist on the other side of that work is not just empowering but can be liberating as well.

Figure 3.3: Opening new doors to fREADom by learning new words. Illustration by Pascale Ife Williams (2023).

Here are some tips I have learned as a teacher and reader about how to break things down as I read:

1. Break down the text into chunks. Use that to set a reading goal for yourself—maybe it's a chapter or

a certain number of manageable pages in a novel. Maybe it's a section under a specific heading, like in an article or a book like this one. Then, feel the success of meeting that goal!

2. Keep the online thesaurus or dictionary a close-by reference. Before doing a close read, skim the lines for the words you don't know and then paraphrase or put them in your own words. A close read is reading to understand each sentence as if it were under a microscope.

3. Highlight the first two sentences of a paragraph and read these closely so that you can get the general idea of the entire text or book that you are reading. This is more helpful for books on history, articles, or books like this one.

4. Reading alone can be great to get into your own thoughts, but reading with someone or a group can also be fun and help with understanding concepts or talking through ideas.

5. Sometimes it takes having a general idea about something before diving deep to learn all the details of something. Googling infographics, or watching a video or documentary, can be a first step towards understanding an issue. That may spark a curiosity that gives you the stamina to read.

6. The truth is, you may be a more auditory learner, which means you learn more by listening. See if your book comes in an audio version. LibriVox is a free app that contains a lot of audio books.

7. Reading a nonfiction book cover to cover is a great way to get in as much information as possible—but it's not always necessary. Often, doing a close read of the intro and conclusion gives you the central argument, insight about how the book is organized, and solutions they want you to take away. Remember, as a **scholar-activist**, you are not only a leader seeking to gain knowledge for the sake of

a test, but you can use it towards some action. Read what you need, check to see if this info is accurate,[2] and keep it moving!

8. Feeling really stuck? Start with autobiographies and memoirs. These can be an interesting way to learn not only about the stories of individuals stepping into their **power**, but the history of the time and place—the historical context—in which they were alive and struggled.

Scholar-activism—as a **principle** of leadership—tells you to see yourself *as* history. It is a **principle** that reminds us that through careful **study**, we all can become a scientist or psychologist of our environments. We can learn the tools to create experiments of **healing** or solutions to problems in our community. This **principle** reminds us that knowledge, like history, is always changing. As we continue to experience global changes, this is an important time to remember our ability to shape the world we want through our thoughts and actions. That includes everything from knowing how **power** has existed in the world, and what **power** we have within it right now. This sets our imagination up for the next chapter, which explores our next TUFF Girls **principle**: to be an **organizer** of your people.

---

[2] Accurate information usually can be seen in at least two other credible sources of information. A "credible source" is a place that holds information (like a website or a book) that you can trust. Generally speaking, this does not include Wikipedia.

Questions for Reflection:

1. School is one place where learning happens. What are the other places in your life that learning happens?
2. When you hear thinking/reading/writing for freedom, what comes up for you?
3. What is a struggle in your life or in your community that you would like to better understand? What questions would you like to ask people to help you better understand them? How else could you learn the answers to those questions? What is stopping you from asking and searching for the answers?

Recommended Reading:

The Bluest Eye, Toni Morrison
Assata: An Autobiography, Assata Shakur
When I Was Puerto Rican, Esmeralda Santiago
For Colored Girls Who Have Considered Suicide When the Rainbow Is Enuf, Nzotake Shange
Pushed Out: The Criminalization of Black Girls, Monique Morris
Black Enough: Stories of Being Young and Black in America, Ibi Zoboi
Little Leaders: Bold Women in Black History, Vashti Harrison
Incidents in the Life of a Slave Girl, Harriet Jacobs
Prison Industrial Complex, James Braxton Peterson
Tell Me Who You Are: Sharing Our Stories of Race, Culture, & Identity, Winona Guo and Priya Vulchi
Black Girls Rock, ed. Beverly Bond
Claudette Colvin: Twice Toward Justice, Phillip Mouse
An Indigenous People's History of the United States, Roxane Dunbar-Ortiz
Red Scarf Girl: A Memoir of the Cultural Revolution, Ji-li Jiang

A Queer History of the United States, Michael
   Brownshi
*They Called Me a Lioness: A Palestinian Girl's Fight for
   Freedom*, Ahed Tamimi and Dena Takruri
*An African American and Latinx History of the United
   States*, Paul Ortiz
Lies My Teacher Told Me: Young Reader's Edition,
   James W. Loewen, adapted by Rebecca Stefoff
Tasting the Sky: A Palestinian Childhood, Ibtisam
   Barakat

Playlist for Scholar-Activism:

"Brown Baby," Nina Simone
"Ancestor's Watching (Chant)," Black Youth Project
   100 Choir
"I Love Being Black," Jonathan Lykes and Black
   Youth Project 100 Choir
"Freedom Side (Chant)," Charlene Carruthers and
   Black Youth Project 100
"I Know I Can," Nas
"Break You Down," Georgia Anne Muldrow
"Dance or Die," Janelle Monae featuring Saul
   Williams
"ABCs of New York," Princess Nokia
"Teacher Don't Teach Me No Nonsense," Fela Kuti
"Lift Every Voice and Song," Boys Choir of Harlem

CHAPTER 4

COMMUNITY ORGANIZER

Every moment is an organizing opportunity, every person a potential **activist**, every minute a chance to change the world.

—Dolores Huerta

TUFF Girls gave me the ability to speak my mind and make others listen. [It] allowed me to be a part of something much bigger than myself and is part of the reason I'm so vocal and free-spirited now.

—Sameera Sullivan, TUFF Girls Leader

I learned [from TUFF Girls] what it meant to be woke . . . and what it meant to fight back and the different ways we can fight back.

—Sophia Delgado, TUFF Girls Teaching Assistant

About a year before I started TUFF Girls, I was in the home of a community **organizer** who had a few jumbo sticky notes on their living room wall. They were left over from a meeting they just had and on one of them was written:

Organizing is having conversations with people that build relationships, connect issues to solutions, and get people to take action, building our **power** in numbers to change systems of **power**.

This was how I envisioned what it meant to turn up for freedom. This is why we read about the Black Panther Party and the Young Lords Party and the ways they fought against **racism**, **capitalism**, and **patriarchy** during the 1960s. TUFF Girls was trying to continue this history by organizing the people in our community to build with each other to transform systems of **power** and their impact on us. To do that well, we were trying to organize our **healing** AND resistance.

So, what does that take? It takes the courage and willingness to take action, internally and externally. Organizing **healing** often asks you to feel uncomfortable before you feel comfortable. Organizing resistance asks you to be courageous enough to look at the root causes of a wound and believe that change is possible. It also asks you to be bold enough to inspire people to do the same, even when you get met with their fears and doubts—or your own. In the seventh or eighth grade, who has the energy for all that? To be honest, even adults feel this tension.

A part of transitioning into young adulthood is experiencing this as a special and hard time. You are learning more about the world, and figuring out who you want to be within it. You want to explore your unique identity, and feel strong inside yourself, but also crave to feel really seen and celebrated by your peers. Or respected and admired for being different but still cool. I get it.

So, to organize your peers around a shared injustice you are experiencing in and out of school may feel scary. Especially if that injustice is calling out **transphobia**, ableism, **patriarchy**, or other **systems of oppression** that benefit some at the expense of others. It may not be safe to do so, especially if you are the only person calling on this injustice or impacted by it. It may also touch on the **ego**, the part of ourselves that wants to be perfect, be in control, and seek outside validation over our own integrity or gifts. Depending on what kind of personal struggles you are having, or what your peers might be experiencing, you might not feel ready for organizing resistance just yet, and that's okay. Courage takes time, and organizing asks you to be brave.

Many of the TUFF Girls did not feel ready either, especially when they were in middle school. Like some of you they were trying to navigate caring for siblings, social and financial insecurities, all while also just wanting to be a kid. Still, most saw themselves in the Black Lives Matter **movement**, the **movement** to end **rape culture**, and the **movement** to interrupt the **school-to-prison pipeline**. Feeling ignited by these racial and **gender justice movements**, TUFF Girls experimented with youth-led **community organizing** by creating **freedom parties**.

Practicing Community Organizing in TUFF Girls

Much of the conversation TUFF Girls were having in that first cycle was about the judgment and violence against girls and cis and **trans** women they saw in their daily life. It was happening in their homes, or around the corner from the center where mostly **trans** women were doing survival work. This inspired a semi-private freedom party where they did a fashion show with a twist—this wasn't about showing off clothes or even showing off their beauty. This was about walking down the runway as freely as they wished they could walk down the street without fear of harassment.

Later that winter, we held our first public freedom party. During this time, it was announced that Darren Wilson—the white police officer who killed Mike Brown, an unarmed Black youth from Ferguson,

Missouri—would not be charged in his death. This was just a few months after the white vigilante George Zimmerman was also not charged in the murder of Trayvon Martin, another unarmed Black youth. Like many young people around the country, Philly students had enough of what felt like the lack of **accountability** of adults who killed Black youth.

TUFF Girls were inspired by the ways Philly high school students were speaking up in their schools by organizing die-ins. These die-ins were a **direct action**, where students interrupted the normal school day and occupied the school hallway by laying down on the floor to show solidarity with the youth who had been victims of police and vigilante violence.

TUFF Girls decided that the main feature of the Freedom Party would be a march. To inspire and educate their peers and other young kids in the neighborhood, they each led different stations in the community center where our program was held. At the stations, people could create signs and make T-shirts or get a freshly made smoothie. There was also a self-care station full of massage balls, aromatherapy lotion, and affirmation cards. TUFF Girls managed stations where there was lots of conversation and relationship building. We had DJ Lovely spinning some music to keep the vibe high!

After about an hour of children and adults going through each station, we held a rally. This was where TUFF Girls shared individual speeches that spoke to the goals of why they were gathering people. It explained their personal relationship to our collective cause and educated people about the shared struggles of Black and Brown girls with Mike Brown and Trayvon Martin. We also lifted up the lives of those children recently killed in North Philly, after a carjacking—and sexual assault of the woman being carjacked—resulted in the car crashing into a candy stand run by a mother along with her children. Mya, our TUFF TA at the time, then led the crowd of nearly forty people in a die-in which lasted for one minute.

Figure 4.1: TUFF Girls leader and teaching assistant Mya leads the group in a die-in, to honor youth killed by the state.

From there, Mya explained that we would be marching through Hunting Park and towards the exact corner where the mother and her children were killed. TUFF Girls led the march with a large banner that said "Walk for **Justice**" framed by the names of Black women and girls killed by the police. They led the crowd with chants, "Hey hey, ho ho, this racist system has got to go!" They also sang a rendition of a chant from Freedom Schools, "Chant down Babylon, Black and Brown youth are the bomb!"

Figure 4.2: TUFF Girls Aisha and Haneefa hold our banner, as we march and chant along 10th Street towards Erie Avenue.

As we walked down 10th Street, then Erie Avenue, and even took to Broad Street, a major street in Philadelphia, neighbors on their porches and in their cars raised their fists. Many shouted out "Black **Power!**" and some honked their horns. There was a spirit of love and pride for these children. Most of the marches at that time took place downtown to really confront city officials. But this march took place in the hood. It let adults know that TUFF Girls and the youth that joined them cared about their lives and about keeping their community safe.

We stopped at the exact location where the mother and her children had been killed just months before. This was just two blocks from where the majority of TUFF Girls went to school. In fact, many of them knew the children killed since they were classmates.

These TUFF Girls were still grieving. We had a local poet, Nina Lyrispect, share a poem called "Young Black America" that reminded us of why we marched. At the end, we released balloons to honor the lives lost and to mark our commitment to never forget them.

Figure 4.3: Nina "Lyrispect" Ball recites her poem at the corner of Germantown Avenue and Allegheny Avenue, where several months earlier a mother and her children were killed during a carjacking that turned into a car crash.

That march was powerful for the people involved, especially for the TUFF Girls who led it. It raised awareness and showed how issues could intersect in unique ways for Black and Brown girls. In a TUFF Girls meeting after the march, youth leaders shared its impact on them:

> *"It felt so freeing to walk down Erie with our signs, chanting, and really being about something."*

"I loved hearing all the people honk for us."
"I liked getting on the megaphone and being loud.
In a good way."
"People don't think kids want to make a differ-
ence or that we care. But we showed them that
we care."

Dr. Shawn Ginwright, a **scholar-activist** and youth worker based in California would say that these reflections show **"radical healing"** at work. TUFF Girls got to experience a sense of freedom inside themselves as they protested racial and **gender** violence and collectively affirmed that Black children matter. Having the adults around them helped them to feel strengthened by their community, and the community felt strengthened by their pursuit for **justice**.

They felt this again as they shared truth to the **power** about **consent** and Black girls' safety at the March to End **Rape Culture** in 2015. And in 2016, when they tied ribbons of their stories of harsh discipline onto the fence of Bethune Elementary on Old York Road. And again in 2018, when they took to the streets with hundreds of their peers on Broad Street in a march led by Philadelphia Student Union and Youth United for Change. After the Parkland shooting, the governor of Pennsylvania and other people from the state legislature were considering bringing more police to schools. They even discussed allowing teachers to carry guns in classrooms to address school shootings. At each march, they brought the message and spirit of the **movement** to the heart of North Philly and they brought North Philly energy to the larger national **movement** for Black lives.

Community organizing isn't only about marches, though. That's one key tactic, but not a **strategy** for sustaining people **power** or creating pressure for change to happen. The difference between a tactic and

strategy is similar to the difference between activism and organizing.

Let's Get Into It: Activism vs. Organizing

The first time I heard of the **activist** vs. **organizer** debate, I was in a gym that had been turned into a safe space for protestors. It was August 13, 2014, several days after eighteen-year-old Michael Brown was shot dead in the street by a police officer who claimed he stole a pack of cigarillos. I was twenty-eight years old. I was there in Ferguson, Missouri on behalf of a national organization called Black Youth Project (BYP) 100 that I helped start that year with nearly 100 Black youth from around the country shortly after George Zimmerman was found not guilty in the shooting of Trayvon Martin, an unarmed Black seventeen-year-old he fatally shot. Along with a few other members, I was moved to join the uprising given all the violent suppression of the Black youth of Ferguson exercising their First Amendment right to "peaceably assemble" in protest. After a day of collaborating with local artists who were offering art **healing** activities to youth in Brown's apartment complex, I sat and listened to my peers argue about the distinct differences between **activists** and community **organizers**. **Activists** were described as the individuals who signed petitions or performed rap songs for an event. That is, **activists** moved as individuals who believed that their leadership was to be "a voice for the voiceless." They were charismatic and **ego**-driven, my peers warned me. I listened with quiet embarrassment. I, too, moved as the kind of **activist** they were talking about.

According to them, a community **organizer** was deeply rooted in the community they were trying to build **power** with. They were concerned with building relationships in order to build up the **consciousness** and leadership of those people most **directly impacted** by the problem. Community **organizers** tried to use that network of leaders to **demand** specific changes from a **target** or person in **power**, who was also connected to the issues at hand.

It was the difference between: (1) getting a street named after Mike Brown; or (2) getting his city council of St. Louis to move some of the money funding its police department to instead fund a program for youth employment. Both were wins, but the second win shifted **power**. The first one created symbolic change that recognized that Mike Brown is a human to be remembered. But the second win was shifting some of the conditions that made it difficult for Mike Brown to live as a young Black boy. For my peers, the first win was seen as *charity* for one person, while the second win was seen as justice for a whole community.

Organizing a **campaign** that shifts **power** takes time and a whole lot of work that goes unseen. It was not a one-person show. The end goal was not to be famous or be the "voice for the voiceless." Youth leaders who have decided to become **organizers** have allowed the work to transform them by listening to what's happening on the ground. They have understood that a true sign of their leadership is moving the so-called voiceless to use their own voices and chant their **demands** in harmony, much like a chorus.

Does that mean that activism is bad?

The root word of activism is to act—and it's often necessary to take some kind of action, especially if people are suffering or being neglected. It can be an important first step in understanding your **power** as an individual. Small acts of kindness and appreciation are the easiest way to feel this.

Most of our marches and **freedom parties** organized by TUFF Girls were short-term experiments in **community organizing**. Without a clear **target** or clear **demands**, our experiments or parties brought up necessary conversations about street harassment, police violence, and racist and sexist judgment of Black and Brown **femmes**. We impacted each other, family members, and some community members. Political education can feel radically **healing** since it offers a sense of self and collective empowerment.

Often, activism is a courageous act that an individual can do by themselves. For example, when I was fifteen, I was a camp counselor. I would read on the school bus, or as a lot of city kids call it, "the cheese bus." It helped me pass the time as we made the hour-long drive from the Bronx to upstate New York. I remember one morning one of my eleven-year-old campers saw me reading and commented, "Books are stupid and boring." Rather than pass judgment (which I did at first), I shared this with my supervisor. I was thinking about doing a book challenge as a way to respond. He had major doubts that any of the girls would do it, since, according to him, reading just isn't a fun thing to do in the summer. I was even more determined to push back, and I think now of what I wasn't aware of then: my white male supervisor might have said that because he had low expectations for Black and Brown kids from the Bronx.

Later that night, I typed up the rules of the challenge, brought in a huge bag of books I had kept from middle school, and would you believe it? The next day all twelve of my campers took a book from the bag! In the end, only about half of them completed the challenge. But, by taking action, I changed the conversation and perception of reading within that small group. Often, that is what activism can do: bring awareness to an issue that may have not even been seen as an issue worth thinking about. I felt proud. Activism can bring that joy as well.

Taking action was me stepping into my leadership in a way that made sense to my fifteen-year-old self at the time. Honestly, I didn't even know that what I did was an act of leadership or a kind of activism. My goal was not to confront my supervisor and hold him accountable for his comment—although I could have. It also wasn't to try and make sure that the camp I worked for had a library full of children's books that reflected the children of the camp—although I could have done that too. I didn't do those things because I didn't have a vision for what I really wanted for the whole camp. I was simply reacting to the negative statements and wanted to show that reading could be fun.

Movement building teaches us that if we want to see deeper change, we will also have to advance our activism into organizing. Intergenerational organizing with children *and* adults builds grassroots **power**, which is important for groups of people who don't have institutional **power**. That means, getting curious about your leadership development and political education, even if you don't join an organization or **community organizing** just yet. This can help you make better choices about where you invest your time, energy, and even your money. You'll know when you are ready and when it's time to lean more deeply into this **principle** of **community organizing**.

Tools for Community Organizing

You know why else it can feel hard to lean into this principle? In the chapter on **healing** and **trauma** I mentioned how the violence of **oppression** on our bodies can rob our imagination for what is possible. If your imagination is narrow based on your experiences of **oppression**, hope can feel far away. That chapter also shared that we have the **power** to support the brain's repair from **trauma**. Taking action through **community organizing** can help build that imagination.

In your Social Studies classes in school, you are likely already learning about one kind of community organizing: voter drives for **civic engagement**. SOUL (School for Organizing, Unity, and Liberation) is an organization that takes it a step further. They train youth **organizers** from around the United States to take collective and strategic action to address injustice in the here and now. They teach the skills to organize a campaign, how to create a vision for what you want, and identify the political education you need to make that vision happen. Philadelphia Student Union is one organization of many that attends these training sessions. Here is a story of one of their rapid-response campaigns when one of their youth **organizers** experienced an injustice at their school.

"Dare to Struggle, Dare to Win: The Story of How Philly Youth Leaders Organized"

In 2016, Brian X was a sophomore at Ben Franklin High School when he was put into a chokehold by a school police officer after attempting to use the bathroom. From the chokehold injury, he experienced a mild concussion. Fortunately, Brian was part of a youth organizing organization called Philadelphia Student Union (PSU). They quickly responded to Brian by organizing. This looked like youth and their adult allies sitting around the table for many hours to create a vision for what they wanted when assaults occur, like the one that happened to Brian. They didn't want this to ever happen again, yet they knew it would.

In that time, they created six **demands** by researching other strategies (remember **scholar-activism?**), identifying Dr. Hite, superintendent of Philadelphia district schools, as the **target**, and developing a plan of action for gaining community support. After several protests in front of the school building, and weeks of pressure from the community—in and outside of Philly—Dr. Hite agreed to meet with them. The meeting included two youth **organizers** from PSU and one adult **ally**, Hiram Rivera, the director of PSU. The rest of the organization stood outside of the building to keep morale up and continue to raise community awareness about why the organization was at the school district building that day. After several hours of fact sharing and testimony, five out of the six **demands** were won. This included the removal of the school officer from Ben Franklin and a complaint system that kept record of complaints against school police officers—the first of its kind in the country.

* * *

Wasn't that a dope win? It's important to share that there is no formula for winning a campaign. Every group has a different set of conditions they are working with. They each have different needs and different relationship dynamics within them to consider. Wherever transformation is happening, though, it is because there is daring to struggle. Black Panther Party member Fred Hampton once said in a speech, "You have to understand that people have to pay the price for peace. If you dare to struggle, you dare to win."[1] Struggle of this kind was a long-term **strategy** for a caring community, collective courage, and political action.

> *Let's check in, my dear: when you think about working with other people, especially people you don't know, what does your body feel? If you feel tense, that's real. That might be old experiences from your past sounding a false alarm. I invite you to take a deep breath. Easy breath in, easy breath out. Get curious about any anxious thought that comes up. Continue softening the body with breath. Ask yourself: who or what do you need to feel tapped into your **power** and ready to build with other people focused on a more just world for everyone? Take your time with this question. Be gentle. Be kind.*

In the Appendix of this book there is a list of organizations around the country that give youth organizing opportunities. I hope you feel encouraged by all the work that people are doing to refuse the status quo and create a more equitable future for us all. May your reading about their work wake up your imagination for conversations that could happen at your school or community center and in your life.

Since there are few radical youth spaces that center Black and Brown girls and **gender-expansive** youth the way that TUFF Girls did, we wanted to also take this time to celebrate them here. We thank them for continuing to sustain young folks in **movement** building around the issues created by **white supremacy**, **patriarchy**, and **capitalism**. We hope that other

---

[1] Fred Hampton, " I Believe I'm Going to Die," *New York Times*, July 21, 1971, *https://www.nytimes.com/1971/07/21/archives/article-1-no-title.html*.

Examples of Community Organizations

Assata's Daughters	A Long Walk Home	Girls for Gender Equity
Led by Black women and operates through a **Black queer feminist lens,** this Chicago-based organization focuses on political education, organizing, and revolutionary services. In October 2015, Assata's Daughters organized a protest at the International Association of Chiefs of Police (IACP) Conference in Chicago. This work continued in their #NoCopAcademy campaign.	Chicago-based A Long Walk Home centers Black girl survivors in middle school and high school through arts activism and political education. Their political education focuses on **healing, consent** culture, and seeks to disrupt the **harm** and cycles of violence associated with **rape culture.**	This NYC-based organization works intergenerationally, through a **Black feminist** lens, to center the leadership of Black girls and **gender-expansive** young people of color in reshaping culture and policy through advocacy, youth-centered programming, and narrative shifts to achieve **gender** and racial **justice.**

Radical Monarchs	Girls Justice League	SOUL Sisters Leadership Collective
A California-based organization that creates opportunities for young Black girls and **gender-expansive** youth of color to form fierce friendships, celebrate their identities, and contribute radically to their communities. They learn about topics like: the **gender binary**, Black-led organizing, and radical forms of collective care and solidarity. They have even taken political action and testified at their local city council meetings.	Open to female-identified youth in the Philadelphia area between ages 13–24. Offers summer training institutes on political education and **community organizing** and an annual conference called Turning Points to share this political education and get support for their campaigns from other youth.	Although they sunsetted in 2022, this Miami-based intergenerational collective was centered on Black girls and **gender-expansive** youth. They received political education and opportunities to support youth organizing in the city and engage in social entrepreneurship.

spaces that center Black girls feel motivated by their radical organizing and love for all the tough girls.

Much of this chapter focused on **community organizing**, since this is how **movements** for environmental, education, **abolition**, **disability justice**, and reproductive justice have been sustained for centuries. Often schools and the media teach about **movements** by looking at individual people. This can erase the fact that change to the status quo and culture requires **movements** of people. The great civil rights **movement** leader Ella Baker taught us that leadership development should focus on group centered leadership, not charismatic leadership. To honor this wisdom, we will close by lifting up individuals whose leadership has inspired different organizations towards **movement** building.

Healing our bodies and protecting each other from **systems of oppression**. Studying our conditions so we can take strategic action and organize our community to do the same. Do you see how each **principle** builds on each other and helps us build a **movement** for freedom? Now as we head into this final **principle**, I invite you to breathe in these words of wisdom from Liberian peace **activist** Leymah Gbowee:

> The road to freedom is long, the cost of freedom is high [and] the fight for freedom is not for the fainthearted and the pessimists.[2]

To keep our spirits high and our hearts strong, and be disciplined in our other **principles**, our final principle was a key source of **power**: to be turnt up for **radical joy**.

---

[2] Karen Leigh and Vivienne Walt, "Nobel Women: The Peace Prize Goes to Three Fighting for Their Rights," *TIME*, October 7, 2011, https://content.time.com/time/world/article/0,8599, 2096450,00.html.

Examples of Community Organizers

Page May	Ella Baker	Rosa Parks
Assata's Daughters began in 2015, when it's founder Page May shared with a group of community members her thoughts around creating a radical space for young Black girls with Assata Shakur being the namesake and north star of the organization. She was also a part of Black Youth Project 100 as well as the Chicago Teachers Union.	Ella Baker mentored Martin Luther King, Jr., along with many youth **activists** in SNCC (Student Non-Violent Coordinating Committee) throughout the 1930s. Her approach to leadership development focused on consensus building and decision making to create grassroots solutions racial and **class** inequality. In this way, she mentored many throughout the civil rights **movement.**	Most people know Rosa Parks for refusing to give up her seat on a bus when it was illegal for Black people to sit at the front of the bus in the Jim Crow South. However, Rosa Parks was a trained **organizer** who had long been part of supporting different battles in defense of Black people, locally and nationally. She also organized a **campaign** to support Recy Taylor after she survived a brutal sexual assault by a group of white men. She founded the "Committee for Equal **Justice** for Mrs. Recy Taylor," which brought national media attention to the Black woman's fight for safety and dignity.

Alicia Garza, Patrice Cullors, Opal Tometti	Elle Hearns	Mariame Kaba
These three Black queer women were already organizing around domestic workers, prison **justice**, and immigrant **justice**, respectively, when they came together after the death of Trayvon Martin. Their affirmation sparked a new generation of **organizers** to make #BlackLivesMatter into a **movement** for change in 2013. This sparked chapters to emerge throughout the United States, as well as around the world.	Elle Hearns is a Black **trans** woman who founded the Marsha P. Johnson Institute to support **trans** leadership in developing services and campaigns to protect the rights and dignity of Black **trans** people. Originally from Columbus, OH, she realized that little was being done to help the Black **trans** community with the violence as well as the job discrimination they were experiencing. She has coached many leaders within the **Movement** for Black Lives on how to center the **trans** experience within the political education of the public.	Mariame Kaba is an abolitionist who trains youth and adults in **transformative justice**. She is co-founder of Project Nia and Interrupting Criminalization. She also works with people to support those who have experienced violence and want to engage the person who hurt them without relying on the police or the court system. She has written books for children and adult audiences on the impact of mass incarceration and what it means to be an abolitionist.

Rasmea Odeh	Charlene Carruthers	mia mingus
Rasmea Odeh is a Palestinian grassroots **organizer** known for working with Arab women in the Chicago area to empower them in their relationships with their partners, help them learn English, and support them with their paperwork (i.e., filing for citizenship, applying for school, etc.). Originally from Palestine, Odeh was also active in resisting Israeli apartheid before she came to the US. Like many Palestinians doing this work, she was targeted, arrested, tortured, sexually abused, and jailed for ten years. After a prisoner exchange, she immigrated to the US. After twenty-three years of organizing in the US and calling for an end to apartheid, she was deported for not mentioning her previous capture in an Israeli prison.	Born in Chicago's South Side, Charlene Carruthers was the first national director of Black Youth Project 100 (BYP100), a national organization fighting for the liberation of all Black people. She supported the leadership development of membership as well as the campaigns of different chapters in Chicago, New York, Detroit, New Orleans, and Durham. In this role, she also supported other organizations focused on the fight against state sanctioned violence, such as the Dream Defenders. Before the founding of BYP100, Carruthers was an active **organizer** in the immigration fight and an advocate for education **justice**.	mia mingus is a queer disabled Korean adoptee who organizes people around **transformative justice** through the Bay Area **Transformative Justice** Coalition. Along with several other people she coined the term "**disability justice**," which centers the needs of disabled people experiencing multiple forms of **oppression**. She also developed the tool of pod-mapping which helps people plan for safety ahead of conflict and crisis by identifying people and spaces that can support in that process.

Questions for Reflection:

1. What comes up in your body when you think about organizing your peers?
2. What fears and excitements do you have about **community organizing**?
3. What are some issues happening in your school that you think deserves a campaign? Who are the people in **power** you and your peers would need to speak with to address it and what support would you need?

Recommended Reading:

Ya'll Tryin' to Win or Nah, Youth United for Change
Doin' The Work, Youth United for Change
Unapologetic: A Black Queer Feminist Mandate, Charlene Carruthers
Hey, Shorty! A Guide to Combating Sexual Harassment and Violence in Schools and on the Streets, Girls for Gender Equity, Joanne Smith, Meghan Huppuch, and Mandy Van Deven
Girls Resist! A Guide to Activism, Leadership, and Starting a Revolution, Kaelyn Rich
You Are Mighty: A Guide to Changing the World, Caroline Paul
Brother, Sister, Leader: The Official Curriculum of The Brotherhood/Sister Sol, Susan Wilcox
A Girl's Guide to Joining the Resistance: A Feminist Handbook in Fighting for Good, Emma Gray
When They Call You a Terrorist: A Story of Black Lives Matter and the Power to Change the World, Patrisse Khan-Cullors and asha bandele
I Got the Light of Freedom: The Organizing Tradition and the Mississippi Freedom Struggle, Charles Payne

Playlist for Community Organizing:

"Ella's Song," Sweet Honey in the Rock
"We Got Power," Tasha (featuring Ethos)
"I Believe That We Will Win," Aflocentric and
    Fresco Steez
"We Gon' Be Alright," Kendrick Lamar
"Fight the Power," Public Enemy
"Black Girl Soldier," Jamila Woods
"Freedom," Beyonce
"Get Free," Makeba
"Get Up, Stand Up," Bob Marley and the Wailers
"Ella Baker Shaker," Big Freedia and Johnathan
    Lykes
"Caskett Pretty," Noname

CHAPTER 5

TURNT UP FOR RADICAL JOY

Joy is the butterfly in the battlefield / . . . is the swingset in the middle of a gun fight / is dodging a bullet / is hopscotch and double dutch / is a fierce gaze, the side eye, the shade / is the sass, snap and the head nod / is the turn up, the swag / joy is righteous and ratchet / joy twerks and taps, jooks and jives / harlem shakes, electric slides, dutty wines / salsas on twos and rumbas / joy is rhythm and repetition[.]

—aja monet, "Black Joy"[1]

I learned to have confidence and try to speak out about things and how I feel. That's what TUFF Girls taught me. I have more confidence than ever. I also learned to never let no one bring you down.

—Haneefa Mahoney Jackson, TUFF Girls leader

I wanted to be in TUFF Girls because I wanted to be loud, in a good way.

—Dyeimah Jackson, TUFF Girls leader

Practicing Being Turnt Up for Radical Joy in TUFF Girls: Getting Loud and Getting Free

At first this **principle** was called "turnt up for life," because turning up for just about anything was the

---

[1] aja monet, "Black Joy," in *My Mother Was a Freedom Fighter* (Chicago: Haymarket Books, 2017).

thing to say in the mid-2010s. Like most cool phrases that come from Black neighborhoods that are most impacted by racial **capitalism** and policing, it spread far enough to mainstream media which then ran it to the ground (boop!). In 2018, the TUFF Girls board replaced it with "**radical joy**"[2] because this more clearly summed up what we were trying to say with "turnt up for life."

Radical joy as a **principle** is the practice of intentionally creating experiences of freedom, child-like joy, and pleasure as you recognize the harmful impact of **systems of oppression**. That last part was what made it radical. Ella Baker taught us that what made something radical was to get at the root of something. **Radical joy** said that we will center joyful activity as we expose the root cause of our pain. This kind of joy can sustain our spirits, without also encouraging us to escape from the reality of our collective experience.

Examples of TUFF Girls practicing **radical joy** have been shared all throughout this book: leaders checking in through circle times and sharing their joy while hearing about someone else's heartbreak; leaders having each other's backs when experiencing **homophobia** and **transphobia**; learning history that helps release the lies learned about them; and yelling chants of truth and affirmation on a bullhorn for everyone in their hood to hear. That is because practicing the other **principles** of **healing, protection, scholar-activism**, and **community organizing** can be challenging work, but the reward is how they help you access **radical joy**. When you read this book again you will see what I mean. For now, allow me to share some

---

[2] *Black joy* in and of itself is radical, because of the centuries of pain and death our lineages have experienced worldwide, simply for existing.

other moments in time at TUFF Girls so you might imagine how else these **principles** helped us access and practice **radical joy**.

Radical Joy inside of Healing

One summer we had a yoga workshop[3] across the street from a playground on 10th Street in the Fairhill section of North Philly where a community member had been killed the summer before. We reflected on how often we don't see children in playgrounds in the hood because of fear and violence. We thought about how **systems of oppression** rob children of public spaces to play and feel the joys of being a child. We then dedicated our session on the mat to that child's life and the safety of our communities. We also set an intention that the peace and **healing** we got for ourselves in our session would flow out into the playground and heal its energy. Together we breathed, we stretched towards each other and towards the sun. We fired up our legs as we practiced balance and connection with the Earth and with our strength. And after savasana, which is the last physical posture where you rest, we all slowly sat up and were beaming with light, smiles, and peace.

Radical Joy inside of Protection

For the majority of our cycles, TUFF Girls decided that their first freedom party would be an overnight

---

[3] I co-facilitated this session with Naima Merella who, like Dr. Sheena Sood and many other radical yogis, talks and writes about decolonizing wellness.

bonding experience, in order to build trust and community, but mostly to have fun. You might remember that for one of our public **freedom parties**, they decided to do a fashion show that raised awareness of **street harassment** by using the runway as a symbol for the street. This became one of their favorite activities to do during the overnight. I think the street is where they and many people are often the most unprotected. We would start out by reminding ourselves that the **systems of oppression** encourage people to harass others in the street about their bodies in ways that try to make them feel shame so the harasser feels a sense of **power** over them. TUFF Girls leaders were then encouraged to walk down the "catwalk" (the hallway of the community center) with pride in their bodies and who they are. The rest of the group would shout affirmations like "I see you!" "Yesssss!" "That's my friend!" We also gave prompts that invited them to express other feelings like anger, sadness, silliness, and nervousness. The affirmations from the group changed with each emotion. Even though some started that walk feeling shy or awkward, by the time they got to the end of the hallway, with the help of the group, they were bubbling with laughter and radiating pride.

Radical Joy inside of Scholar-Activism

In 2013, much of the conversation about twerking danced between Miley Cyrus inventing this and Black girls not having any respect for themselves when they uploaded twerking videos of themselves onto YouTube. The message underlying all of this was that twerking was very sexual, degrading, and invented by a white woman. In response, some schools went so far as to ban twerking altogether and even had students sign a contract saying they wouldn't twerk. At TUFF Girls we acknowledged that dance and movement offered a sense of freedom for many, and we wanted to both correct the history of twerking, while naming some things to consider for safety.

We talked about Katherine Dunham, a Black anthropologist, dancer, and civil rights **activist** of the 1930s who studied the dances of people throughout the African diaspora. While she didn't discuss twerking specifically, she noticed that throughout the Caribbean and the countries of Africa, most cultures engaged the hips, and even isolated movement of the hips. The function or meaning behind this form in most cases was not sexual. In some cases, this was associated with the fertility of the land and a part of rituals for farming; in other cases, it was demonstrating the powerful energy of feminine sensuality more broadly.

As we shared this, we talked about how European dance did not engage the hips at all because of their puritanical and conservative views about **sex** and associating any movement of the hips with it. We reflected on how special it was for Black people to preserve their cultural ways of dance through slavery, even as slavery created the stereotype that Black people were sexually aggressive and thus not human or pure. Given the risks and consequences that come with this sexualization, we talked about the Internet as an unsafe place, and other safe places to engage in dancing, like twerking. So, of course, to honor the African roots of twerking and TUFF Girls as a safer place to express the body, we ended our class with dancing, cheers, and an abundance of **radical joy**. TUFF Girls spread this information through the center and before we knew it, other girls would come to the dance studio knowing that this was a safe space to get free in their bodies.

Radical Joy in Community Organizing

Our final cycle in TUFF Girls was in 2020. For the first time, our meeting spot was not inside of a building, but on an urban farm located in North Philly, across the street from a playground and the Fairhill Apartments housing projects. It was also across the street from where one of our TUFF Girls was hit in a drive-by shooting several weeks before the cycle began. Luckily for us and the world, she survived.

On the farm, we studied the systems of **capitalism, patriarchy**, and **white supremacy** that created the conditions for the gun violence our leaders had to witness and experience. The other goal was to grow **healing** herbs that we would then share with the community as we helped the farm's food distribution to its neighbors.

This was the first summer during the COVID-19 pandemic. The farm was located in a neighborhood impacted by **food apartheid** which meant that if accessing healthy food before the pandemic was challenging, it was even more difficult during it. Between the stress of food scarcity, extreme heat, wearing masks, and the spotted lanternfly invasion, it felt like the end of times. Much of the **community organizing** at the time was centered on mutual aid[4] to get people what they needed, including us.

For TUFF Girls, **radical joy** was in the gratitude that neighbors flooded them with as they walked food boxes to their cars or loaded up their shopping carts. It was watching their herbs grow over time on

---

[4] Mutual aid organizing is a form of organizing that has a long history among many different communities learning to survive scarcity caused by capitalism, displacement, anti-Blackness, and homophobia and transphobia.

two acres of land, especially after a big rain. Smelling their sweet aromas as they harvested them. Turning their plants into medicinal hair oils, body creams, and bath bombs. It was feeling the loving energy they poured into their herbs, returning to them as they caressed their scalp and their skin with the medicine they made. And every time someone from the community purchased their medicine, not only did they bask in **radical joy**, but so did the land from which it grew.

Figure 5.1: TUFF Girls Najah, Renesha, Jazcitty, Gigi, and SynClaire at Life Do Grow Farm in North Philly, 2020.

Let's Get Into: Radical Joy and Pleasure as a Portal to Freedom

What happens to your body when you hear the words **radical joy**, freedom, and pleasure? I invite you to take a deep breath each time you think of each word. For Black writer and **organizer** adrienne maree brown, a part of getting free is also tending to our relationship with pleasure. She calls this "pleasure activism." Like the work of **radical joy**, pleasure activism is "the work we do to reclaim our whole, happy, and satisfiable selves from the impacts, delusions, and limitations of **oppression** and/or supremacy."[5] She has a set of eight **principles** which may feel helpful as you grow your joy practice and consider the politics of feeling good:

1. What you pay attention to grows.
2. We become what we practice.
3. Yes is the way.
4. When I am happy, it is good for the world.
5. The deepest pleasure comes from riding the line between commitment and detachment.
6. Make **justice** and liberation feel good.
7. Your no makes the way for your yes. (**Boundaries** create the **container** within which your yes is authentic.)
8. Moderation is key.

What I love about these **principles** is they help us to consider juicy ways we can bring pleasure and **radical joy** to practicing the **principles** of **healing, protection, scholar-activism**, and **community**

---

[5] adrienne maree brown, *Pleasure Activism: The Politics of Feeling Good* (Chico: AK Press, 2019), 13.

Figure 5.2: Principles of pleasure activism by adrienne maree brown. Illustration by Pascale Ife Williams (2023).

organizing. They also help us to consider that pleasure shouldn't be doing whatever you want to feel good, if it hurts yourself or others. That it can help feed **systems of oppression** and lead to more suffering or even death. It is a practice of staying connected to our bodies without being led by our impulses or emotions. With so many things that offer pleasure— food, art, dancing, community, being restful, just to name a few—there are many opportunities to practice pleasure activism.

Exploring Pleasure through the Body

Even though TUFF Girls learned about **rape culture** and felt great pride and joy in being speakers at the March to End **Rape Culture** in 2015, we never had in-depth discussions about **sex** as an act of pleasure between two people consenting to sexual activity. We also never talked about pleasure activism. I want to address it here, especially as you journey through middle school and high school, where you may receive a lot of mixed messages and misinformation about **sex**.

If this topic makes you feel uncomfortable, that's real too. Give yourself what you need to be ready to come back with an open mind. That might mean doing a bit of writing or talking to a friend in order to help process why talking or reading about **sex** makes you uncomfortable. Keep in mind, some of this might be because adults and youth tend to shame certain youth who ask questions or talk about **sex**. Under **patriarchy** and **transphobia**, only cis boys are allowed to talk about and explore desire for cis girls.

For those who are perceived as girls and/or identify as such, they are talked about as "fast" or "too grown," instead of wanting to learn about the human experience. For those who are curious or confident about their **gender** outside of the **gender binary**, such as **nonbinary** and **trans** youth, they may experience being made an outcast by their peers and the adults in their lives. Any youth who has had their **boundaries** violated at an early age and has not had a chance to process that pain may actually be more curious or take more risks at an earlier age. All these young folks need **healing** and support, not judgment, isolation, or violence.

Sometimes, judgments from adults are actually fears that have been passed down from slavery, when Black children were even more vulnerable to being the victims of sexual assault. These fears may also be the result of **generational trauma**, where the psychological stressors of one generation of a family are passed onto the many generations after it. Adults are often hoping to protect you from the pain of being sexualized young and we don't always understand how to best help you. For many of us, we are still processing our own **traumas** from childhood. All of this is part of the history of why this has been a hard conversation to have and why they don't always go well when they finally happen.

The other harsh reality for some of our youth is that they don't have trustworthy and dependable caregivers. Many youth who identify as queer and **trans** are kicked out of their homes, forcing them to learn how to survive. Other predatory adults might promise safety, money, or approval to unhoused youth, and once they have gained their trust, start to **harm** and/or exploit them for their own benefit or profit. In each case, these youths need support and understanding from the people around them, and from themselves.

Here are some things to consider as you are exploring pleasure and learning what it means to step into your **power** in an intimate relationship. Hopefully it helps the conversation around pleasure feel less difficult or uncomfortable.

1. *Explore your own sexual curiosities and pleasures with yourself, by yourself, first and foremost.* In other words, masturbation is one way to learn yourself that is often not discussed. Masturbation looks and feels like many different things for youth of different **genders**. It is a physical act with the body that brings a person towards sexual arousal. What would it mean to learn and grow compassion for all of your body, including your genitalia (also known as private parts, vulva, penis, etc.)?

   The feeling of discomfort is likely to feel stronger if your culture or religion sees masturbation as wrong, if your genitalia doesn't match your **gender** identity, or if you have experienced sexual violence. Understand that this is normal and can change as you spend more personal time being compassionate with yourself and creating a healthy story around this part of yourself. This process will be helpful to **healing** your relationship with the body and with your overall confidence.

Looking at your intimate areas might be really hard. When I was sexually assaulted, I had a hard time looking at my vulva and not crying or feeling sad. One of my dear friends who is a **trans** man said that at one point in time, he had also avoided looking down there, because it was a painful reminder of the disconnect between how he saw himself and how his family saw him. This is all real. Take your time. Be patient. Be tender. Be curious about what comes up. Make a joke when you can. Let some tears out. And remember that there is so much **power** in just sitting with yourself and being a good friend to yourself as you do this.

Educate yourself on the names of your body parts. They don't make you who you are, but they are a part of your flesh. To love yourself is to also learn how to practice gentle compassion with your body. Loving yourself is a superpower.

Lastly, it's also okay to not like masturbation. Nothing is wrong with you if you don't. You may have to spend a bit of time exploring what self pleasure looks like for you. Maybe it's what you daydream about, or what you read or write in the privacy of a safe space. There are so many possibilities. Just be safe and responsible with your body as you get creative in your thinking.

2. *Have courageous conversations.* Speaking of being safe and responsible, if you're considering physical and sexual intimacy, develop the confidence to talk about **consent**. **Consent** is another word for permission. **Consent** should be enthusiastic. If you are hesitating, then you should probably slow down. Also, just because you give **consent** on Monday

doesn't mean you automatically give it again on Tuesday. It should be a nonverbal and verbal agreement; meaning if you say yes, but your body says no, you and the other person should pause.

Gaining **consent** builds trust, but there can be a lot of mixed signals and messages about **consent** if there is no courageous conversation happening. This is true whether you are exploring with someone of the same or different **gender**. There are many ways to experience pleasure with another person that doesn't involve sexual activity (i.e., holding hands, long hugs, back massage, kissing, etc.)—and all of them require **consent**.

In my experience as a youth worker, sexual activity in middle school usually didn't end well because folks were not emotionally ready to deal with the consequences during and after being intimate. Often, folks were engaging in sexual acts out of guilt, pressure, and manipulation. This is true even for some people in high school. If this is you, please know I don't want you to feel shame for this. Rather, I hope you can practice self-forgiveness if and when things don't turn out well. Consider this: what was the lesson learned for the future?

If the person who you are thinking about is much older than you, ask yourself, "Why is this person not dating someone their own age?" Children under sixteen cannot give **consent** to adults, and this is considered sexual assault under law, even if you want to give **consent**. Sadly, many adults, usually cis men, prey on young girls by saying they are "mature for their age," when in reality, it is they themselves who are immature and/or sick. They are manipulating young girls to get what they want. Manipulation is when a person uses a lie to convince you to do something for their own interest, not yours. Remember those child-adult **power dynamics** we talked about in Chapter 1?

If you are exploring sexual intimacy, here are some of the important questions to ask the other person before you do so:

- I am not willing to do _____. How can I trust you will honor those **boundaries**?
- Have you done this before and what does this mean to you?
- How are we doing this safely?
- If I say, "nah, I'm good" during the middle of us being together, how do you think you will react or feel?
- I'm not comfortable with people knowing my business. Who will you likely want to talk to about this with?

Even if you have been sexually active before and didn't ask these questions, you can still ask them. Ideally, you AND the other person are patient with these questions and the awkwardness that can come with them in the beginning. If the other person makes you feel silly or shameful for asking these questions, that is a major red flag. It may be a sign of their lack of maturity or their inability to have an honest conversation about sensitive topics. It might reveal they are only interested in meeting their own desires and don't actually care about yours, including your desire to feel safe. Either way, hit the brakes! That person is not ready for you, and you also may not be ready.

3. ***Look out for red and green flags.*** **Sex** can be both pleasurable and scary. Without preparation and difficult conversations it can also be painful— physically and emotionally. **Sex** is only **sex** when both people say yes and agree on how to do that safely. Research different ways to access protection

from sexually transmitted infections (STIs). Most important: have the courage to advocate for yourself when you might experience pressure, or worse, manipulation. Here are some examples and some ways you can respond where you don't give up your **power**.

What manipulation can sound like	Ways you can hold your power
You aren't a little girl, are you?	I'm old enough to know when I need more time and when I'm not feeling safe or heard.
You're my girlfriend, right? This is what you are supposed to do.	Being your girlfriend doesn't mean I abandon myself. I want a partner who understands that.
It's not that big of a deal.	If it's not that big of a deal to you, then you won't be upset when I say I'm good. Also, it's a big deal to me. Us not being on the same page about it doesn't make me think this will be a good experience.
I love you. Don't you love me?	Real love won't ask me to betray myself. What are other ways we can show love that makes us both feel good?

It's okay if you respond with a shaky voice at first, or if once you speak your truth then they leave. It's okay to say yes on Friday and then say no on Monday. You are not being mean or selfish. You are learning the hard truth that that person may not be ready to care for you in this very intimate experience. Here are some examples of green-flag responses.

Green-flag responses	Responses that name your boundaries
Are you sure you want to do this? You seem nervous.	Thanks for noticing. I am nervous, and I think I need to talk some things out first.
Does this feel good for you?	Actually, it doesn't. Let's take a break.
As we get to know each other more, I'm curious about your **boundaries**.	I love that you asked. They may change day to day, but right now I feel comfortable with just holding hands.
Even though you are telling me you're fine with this, you don't seem enthusiastic about it, so let's pause on going further.	Thanks for paying close attention to what is going on with me. I really like you and was worried I would disappoint you if I said no. This makes me respect you so much more.

Green flags include: a willingness to be patient and take things slow; they initiate conversations about emotional and physical safety; you feel a sense of care and respect when you name your **boundaries**. Learning to stand in your truth in all moments, including intimate ones, will help you to become a well-rounded leader.

Tools for Practicing Radical Joy

In many ways, TUFF Girls were able to experience **radical joy** by practicing the other **principles. Healing** yourself, protecting others, learning the truth about history and reality, and organizing for change are acts of resistance in an oppressive world that profits from human disconnection. These **principles** helped us to cultivate connection within ourselves, and radical new connections between each other.

And, as we brought **radical joy** to practice these **principles**, it helped us balance fun and pleasure with our community and political work. It often meant going back to the things that brought us pleasure as a smaller child—running around outside, playing games, dancing, coloring, painting, singing, etc. These were things you did before television and social media convinced you and generations of people that certain toys and clothes or certain bodies were better. You are most likely practicing this **principle** already, you just may not have included it as a part of what grows your magic and **power** for leadership.

To help you bring **radical joy** into the work, there are lots of tools for practicing **radical joy** in the book's Appendix, starting at page 165. There are so many that I categorized them by how they bring joy to your mind through more mental activities; or how they may bring joy to your body through more physical activities; and lastly, for how they may bring joy to your spirit through more soulful rituals.

I do want to offer one tool for practicing **radical joy** here, especially if you aren't feeling motivated to access joy. You might feel that way for many reasons. You might be grieving or feeling angry, numb, or like the things that once brought you joy just don't do it anymore. Big hugs, friend. This is an important time for you to sit with your **inner child**.

Inner Child Meditation

You might be saying to yourself, what is an **inner child** if I am still a child? Your **inner child** is simply your younger self. Your younger self might have been more curious, open, and trusting. As life happened, you may have experienced loss, abandonment, rejection, or harsh feedback which encouraged you to become more closed off. Does this sound familiar?

One way to get in touch with this **inner child** is to take your favorite picture from your childhood and sit in a quiet place, like the bathroom. You might even light a candle with the intention of quieting your mind and bringing tenderness to this picture. Take several deep breaths in, and several deep breaths out. Sit with the picture and place one hand on your heart. Listen to what your **inner child** might be asking you.

Share affirmations out loud to that young child that you wish you had received then. Listen to what they need now. This is a loving way to make your **inner child** feel seen and to make yourself feel more whole.

Questions for Reflection:

1. When you have experienced **radical joy**, where were you, what were you doing, who were you with, and how did you feel about yourself?
2. What kind of self-touch feels soothing? Joyful? Pleasurable? If self-touch doesn't bring you any of those emotions, what does it bring? If it brings you shame, where do you think you learned that from?
3. Review the tools for **radical joy** in the Appendix. Which tools would you feel comfortable leading and practicing with a group of your peers?

Recommended Reading:

Trans+: Love, Sex, Romance and Being You, Karen Rayne and Kathryn Gonzalez

The Body is Not an Apology: The Power of Radical Self-Love, Sonya Renee Taylor

Dear Universe: Letters of Affirmation & Empowerment for All of Us, Yolo Akili

The Prophet, Khalil Gibran
The Alchemist, Paulo Coelho
Pleasure Activism: The Politics of Feeling Good,
    adrienne maree brown

Playlist for Turnt Up for Radical Joy:

"Hype for Black Youth Project 100" (chant)
"Show Me Love," Robyn S.
"Level Up," Ciara
"The Kids Are Alright," Chloe x Halle
"Already," Beyonce, Shatta Wale, and Major Lazer
"Spirit," Beyonce
"Holy," Jamila Woods
"Higher," Tems

CONCLUSION

We need to protect dreamers, we need to protect kids in the most vulnerable areas, we need love and for people to care about their communities.

—Mari Copeny

Daily affirmations to remind yourself of who you are . . . so that you *know* who you are. Affirmations helped me a lot. School is a big struggle for me. But if I go in with that mindset, it's going to affect me in the day. But if I go in with an affirmation then I'm going in very differently.

—Najah Whitehead, TUFF Girls leader

If you were born and raised in the United States, you were most likely told that this is the best place in the world to live because you can experience "*real* freedom" here. In fact, many politicians call this country "the land of the free." Some of you might have questioned that, though. You are more likely to do so if you are **nonbinary** or **trans** and have had to watch people and politicians question and attack your existence. You might also question it if you can't walk down the block without strangers talking disrespectfully about your body or giving you unwanted sexual attention. Or, if you have lived in a neighborhood where people struggle to find work, healthy food to eat, quality housing, or safe schools. Because of this, there might also be people in this neighborhood or in your family who have made bad choices out of desperation and are now caged in a prison. This can't be freedom, you think. And you are absolutely right. It's not.

You know that it's not if you know anything about political prisoners, like Mumia Abu Jamal, incarcerated for their political beliefs in Black liberation. For over thirty years an international movement to free him has been ongoing because we know the state is trying to make an example out of him, and we refuse this injustice.

In some of your history classes, you might have even learned that this country has harmed many other countries in order to benefit a small group of rich people in the US. This is the result of **imperialism**. If your school has not taught this history, check out the mini-profiles of the Congo, Haiti, Puerto Rico, and Cuba which you can access in our free toolkit online at the following website: https://tuffgirls215.wordpress.com/. The US government also has a history of supporting countries who **abuse** other countries through force, the way Israel currently does with Palestine. This is why being in solidarity with communities around the world, otherwise known as "internationalism," is so important. The future of humanity and our planet depends on it.

The thought of solidarity on such a large scale might inspire you to action or it might make you shrink. Or both. Believe me, I have been there, and return to that tension more times than not. Let's take a nice slow inhale through the nose, fill the belly, and slowly sigh it out.

The TUFF Girls **principles** recognize that under **white supremacy, capitalism, patriarchy, transphobia**, and ableism, the body is not completely free—not from public judgment, family or community violence, or decisions by the government. This can easily make you a prisoner of insecurity, doubt, or fear.

This is also why **healing** is the first **principle**, so that you can resist negative forces that encourage negative thinking or even make you question your existence. The **principle** of **protection** encourages you to bring this **healing** work into your relationships as you navigate conflict. **Scholar-activism** reminds you that studying our history and conditions help us to understand the root causes of the impact of oppressive conditions. **Community organizing** fires us up to collectively address and transform these conditions. And centering **radical joy** sustains us as we practice these **principles**, even as the **principles** help us to access **radical joy**. In this way, each **principle** is a portal to deeper freedom inside, and together they offer the guidance for a path towards building a **movement** for collective freedom; a path that our freedom-fighting **ancestors** have been journeying for centuries.

* * *

There was once a very smart and passionate Black girl named Tarana Burke who lived in the Bronx; the Highbridge area to be exact. She loved learning history and listening to all the latest hip-hop. When she was seven years old, an older boy in the area forced himself onto her, sexually, causing a deep wound that she kept to herself for a long time. As she got older, however, she found the courage to tell her story to a trusted adult and take small steps towards **healing**. Later, she began working with young girls to create safe spaces of joy and acceptance. As the girls got more comfortable, one by one they shared their wounds with the woman. She listened carefully to their stories, nodding her head. "Me too," she thought, and soon after, said it out loud. Eventually, she recognized this phrase, "me too," was more than just words. It was a powerful invitation for empathy between survivors, and an opportunity to create the community necessary for **healing**.

On October 15, 2017, a tweet went viral overnight where the phrase "me too" was also used as an invitation for solidarity between survivors. Alyssa Milano, a white actress who wanted to increase awareness of sexual **harm** in Hollywood, encouraged her followers to tweet #MeToo if they had experienced such **harm**, and to include their story if they felt comfortable. Twelve million people from around the world answered the call. Tarana was one of them.

Through social media she was able to connect with Milano and provide important context for everyone: working **class** and cash-poor Black girls and women, like the ones she had been working with in Selma, Alabama, who had much less racial and economic **privilege** than white celebrities, experience this **harm** earlier, more often, and with much less support. This is even more true for **trans** youth. For that reason, we need to bring our **resources** and attention towards centering them. How do we create safety and **protection** for them, and for all of us?

The historic victory in this coming together of the minds was the mainstream awareness of a global **movement** that had already been burning on for centuries, long before Tarana Burke's work and Alyssa Milano's tweet. The media was finally beginning to give attention to a very big problem that was swept under the rug for people of all **classes** and racial backgrounds. For more and more people, that experience of sexual **harm** would no longer be a secret they carried to their graves.

Tarana's story teaches us that we grow in our leadership when we make the choice to connect our struggles and strengths with others and believe that building **power** can create transformation. She reminds us that individually we are resilient, but together we can move the culture towards the future we want.

She also teaches us that practicing TUFF Girls **principles** takes time, patience, and compassion. The media started to describe this moment as the **#MeToo movement**, but not because Tarana called the TV stations. It did so because Tarana was not seeking to feed the **ego**, but rather, the collective heart of survivors worldwide. She was able to merge her influence with Milano's and other people's convictions and create a dialogue that built a bridge of understanding.

This would ignite a cross-racial **movement** that inspired survivors of all **genders** to step into their **power** and deepen our understanding of **rape culture** as a product of institutional *and* interpersonal violence.[1] As a result, we saw shifts in policy, cis men with a history of assault and harassment being held accountable in and out of court, and more financial support for community organizations dedicated to supporting survivors and ending **rape culture**, much like the organization she started in 2006. Most importantly, more conversations in our homes and around the world were happening about supporting survivors of sexual **harm** and taking action to prevent more **harm** from happening.

I'm so grateful and proud to say that I worked for two years at the organization that Tarana was able to start in 2017: me too. International. In my role as their program coordinator, I was able to pour my energies into the leadership development of survivors, young and old, as they continue the lifelong journey of **healing**, breaking cycles of violence, and stepping into their collective **power**. In so many ways, I got to bring every single **principle** of TUFF Girls into the

---

[1] A great example of this can be found in the protest song "*Un violador en tu camino*" ["A Rapist in Your Path"] by Chilean feminist collective LASTESIS that went viral in 2019. In the song, they call out the state for being rapist.

work, encouraging survivors to be **healers, protectors, scholar-activists,** community **organizers,** and turnt up for **radical joy.** The overlap between the work of TUFF Girls and 'me too' is not unique. This is the work of *every* organization and group of people wild enough to continue a legacy of refusing to accept the **oppression** of our people.

Oppression, and all of its violence, can shrink our imagination. Hopefully this book reminds you of the tools you have within you, and outside of you, to build that imagination for a safety and kind of **justice** we have not yet felt or seen before. Change is possible when we have big dreams for what is possible. We deserve safe and supportive homes and schools, access to health care that keeps our family well, foods that keep us nourished, housing that provides shelter, and most importantly, we deserve the opportunity to have our individual and collective dreams become reality.

Dear Black and Brown **trans** and cis girls, especially the *tough girls*: you all have taught me that your freedom dreams are some of the most important to protect and nourish. It is your freedom that can help free us all. I have learned that you are the most vulnerable to the **systems of oppression** that adults have maintained for far too long. How you awaken your collective **power** depends on your **healing** and organizing work. Remember, none of you ever do this work alone. This is a global fight. And of course, our enlightened **ancestors** are there, right alongside you, whenever you call them by name.

As we wrap up, I invite you to ground yourself in affirmations, a practice that was among the favorites in TUFF Girls. This is a ritual to get into your body and into the mindset to step out into the world from a place of **power,** despite its attempt to convince you of the opposite. It is something you can do as you prepare to leave for school in the morning or any moment you feel alone or disconnected. Seeds to plant within yourself that you can water over time.

I encourage you to sit in a comfortable seat, or lay down, or to look at yourself in a mirror. Place your left hand on your heart and your right hand on your belly. Take a deep breath and say this out loud:

I am a **healer**.
I am a **protector**.
I am a **scholar-activist**.
I am an **organizer**.
I am **radical joy**.
I am TUFF, and with community, we will all get free.

AFTERWORD

SynClaire Arthur
former TUFF Girls teaching assistant

When I think about my high school experience, one particular moment always stands out. At the time, Vine was a social media platform that was fairly new although quite popular. Peers of mine chose to create a vine during which they recorded themselves sitting around a lunch table, and each took turns saying the word "nigger." They labeled the video "Black people." A friend—another Black girl—and I came across this video and were upset by it, disturbed even. The choice to record and upload the video, along with the behavior and expressions captured in it, made it clear to us that its participants thought their use of the word was a joke.

We thought differently; so we reported it. During our conversation with one of the school's administrators, he concluded that he could not take disciplinary action against the students simply because we were offended. He even likened our experience of coming across the video and being upset by it to his toddler daughter seeing Barney on the television screen and becoming upset by the image and crying. However, he did share that he could and would suspend each student due to using their phones during school hours because it went against school policy. I remember that conversation and moment so vividly because I remember how it made me feel: disappointed; angry; not heard. I found it to be a sad thing that my school had policies to enforce control of student behavior but did not have policies that encouraged respect and **protection** of these same students. I imagine this has been the unfortunate case for many of your schools, too.

But for all the upsetting emotions that experience brought, I reference it because it prompted my friend and I to act. We experienced an injustice and were driven to speak out and say, "this thing is not right." We didn't necessarily get the response from administrators that we wanted but we did feel supported by other members of our school community. In particular, there was one teacher who made space in her classroom for us to facilitate discussions with other students about the incident. Not every student agreed with us, but some did. And for those who didn't, it was eye-opening, and we gained important understandings of the many different positions and opinions people can have on an issue.

I am certain that the video, our response to it, and my high school's response to it contributed to my curiosity and interest in social issues. It's why I chose to take Education for Liberation, a course offered at my college, and which also happened to be taught by Dr. E. The class was a space for me to nurture this curiosity and deepen my understanding of myself, a young Black woman, and my experience in the world as such.

As I embraced the journey unfolding before me, I had the opportunity to support other Black and Brown girls in theirs. My introduction to TUFF Girls was as a teaching assistant, but it is important for me to note that like the girls in the program, I was also learning and growing. That's exactly what made the experience so special. In my role, I was tasked with teaching, but I didn't assume that the girls were incapable of doing the same. I didn't carry the belief that just because I knew what I was doing meant that the girls knew nothing at all. Prior to that moment, I had not witnessed or imagined the possibility of adults acting as allies to youth. But once I did, it changed how I approached youth and others in my studies and my work.

As you read *Turn Up for Freedom*, I hope you are receptive to the wisdom within the stories shared. I also hope that you are inspired and empowered to create change where you want and need it. Most of all though, I hope you feel seen and in a way that you, too, can't resist the desire and need to turn up for freedom for yourself, your people, your schools, and your communities.

APPENDIX

These are additional **resources** to help you to practice the TUFF Girls **Principles** for Leadership. You can find more of our free toolkit online, https://tuffgirls215.wordpress.com/.

I. Resources for Healing and Protection

Safety Plans

A safety plan is a great tool that you can create and keep in your wallet or inside your bookbag. The goal is to reflect and name what triggers you to be angry or sad, identify the things that help you to calm down, and figure out who are the people you can call on in your school or at home. You can put this information on an index card and you can get really creative in putting it together. Use colors and images that are soothing.

Sample Safety Plan Template	
My triggers: These are specific and unique things that cause you to feel unsafe, very anxious, or threatened	*What grounds me:* These are things that help calm you and restore a sense of physical and emotional safety
My go–to people: These people are able to listen and help you to come back to a grounded place	*My mantra:* These are words or affirmations you can tell yourself in a moment of distress

Dr. E's Safety Plan	
My triggers: Blaming victims for their **trauma**, men talking over me or speaking abusively, being interrupted or talked down to	*What grounds me:* Deep breathing, burning palo santo, writing, a glass of water, child's pose, prayer
My go-to people: My best friend, my cousin, my partner, my therapist	*My mantra:* "On the other side of your healing work is your **power**."

II. Resources for Scholar-Activism

The next section will give a brief overview of what is the African diaspora. We shared this history with TUFF Girls leaders so they could better understand the history of how their people came to this land and how that history shapes the conditions we are experiencing today. In our toolkit, we have short historical profiles of several countries of the African diaspora. You are encouraged to always do your own research to better understand this history and the ways you can support the ongoing resistance of these peoples, for wherever there is **oppression** there is always resistance.

Brief History of African Diaspora

A people without the knowledge of their past history, origin and culture is like a tree without roots.
—**Marcus Garvey**

For centuries historians have told us that we all originate from the continent of Africa. As humans chose to migrate, they adapted physiologically to their surrounding environments. Conflict and war over territory, resources, and trade deals impacted many societies. During the 1600s, a smaller band of Europeans took to a spirit of greed and dominance to explore and conquer the world for their own benefit. This is what started the **transatlantic slave trade**, and the 35,000 voyages where Europeans forced or kidnapped Africans (mostly from West Africa) to the Americas. In a few cases, as was the case with certain African chiefs in the Congo, these men traded their people with European slave traders and were aware of the brutal conditions they would be forced to face. This is an early example of the **harms** of Black **capitalism**, where profits come before people, including your own.

Slavery had existed prior to the **transatlantic slave trade**, but "chattel" referred to how Black people were seen as nonhuman. That difference is what made this slavery so brutal. Only one-third of all Africans would be forced into chattel slavery in the United States. The remaining two-thirds would go to Caribbean islands like Puerto Rico, Jamaica, Cuba, Guyana, the Dominican Republic, Haiti, and other parts of Central/South America (e.g., Mexico, Honduras, Panama, Venezuela, Columbia). An even larger number of Africans went to Brazil, which to this day, continues to be home to the highest number of Black people outside of the continent of Africa. During this time, and even well before this time, Africans also traveled to parts of the world for spiritual pilgrimages and discovery, hence, we have seen Black people in places like Palestine and other parts of the Middle East. Sadly, the majority of Black folks were there due to the slave trade within the Ottoman Empire.

Part of the legacy of slavery is accepting **white supremacy**, or **anti-Blackness**. **White supremacy** is the idea that whiteness is the standard for all things true, right, and beautiful. It is how white Christian slave masters **justified** their violence on Black people. **Anti-Blackness** is the rejection of Black people as whole human beings and the rejection of Blackness as true, right, and beautiful. This can be everything from beauty standards, to how one speaks and thinks, and even how one thinks about communities of color. If you are not fully aware of your history, you will not understand that believing that whiteness is better is how *mental slavery* continues.

One of the harsh realities of US slavery was the massive and **systematic** sexual assault of African people, particularly those who could bear children. The children of these assaults would still be enslaved, but would have lighter skin, favoring the genes of the slave master. Lighter-skinned girls/women who were enslaved were granted access to the "big house," and in many other ways received better treatment. At the same time, they were also more vulnerable to nightly sexual attacks and more surveillance.

Part of the legacy of **white supremacy** is that some Black people—darker and light-skinned—help to play out is **anti-Blackness**. This works in the favor of light-skinned Blacks, which is why it is important for them to be critical of **white supremacy**'s impact on them. In a similar way, other people of color—like Arabs, South Asians, Latinos, despite their African ancestry or darker skin—may also believe in and play out **anti-Blackness**. This may look like being harsher or less forgiving of darker-skinned people. They may believe in the stereotypes about dark-skinned people that come out of slavery—such as, they are not beautiful or should take on more labor; they are more violent or sexually fast, and their freedom is seen as a threat to social order. This, too, is the afterlife of slavery.

Many of us often forget or do not know that US slavery ended in 1863, which was late compared to countries like France and England. Many enslaved Africans were not told that they were free well after laws had changed, and in some parts of the Caribbean slavery didn't become illegal until the 1890s. The work available for newly freed Black people was still very similar to the conditions of slavery for a long time. We were enslaved in this country longer than we have been "free." In other words, we are still learning what it means to be free. High unemployment, housing insecurity, harsher prison sentences for Black and Brown people, oversexualization of Black and Brown youth—these realities continue to challenge what our freedom looks and feels like without "chains."

While slavery is technically illegal, it still exists today in the form of prison labor. This means that we need youth leadership who understand this and work to protect each other from all kinds of "chains"—whether they are symbolic or real.

III. Resources for Community Organizing

Directory of Youth Organizations within the USA			
Youth organization	Mission of organization	Location	Social media + website
African Bureau for Immigration and Social Affairs (ABISA)	Promotes social and economic justice, civic participation and empowerment of African immigrants and refugees.	Detroit, MI	https://www.facebook.com/TheAfricanBureau/
A Long Walk Home	Empowers young artists and **activists** to end violence against all girls and women. We advocate for racial and **gender** equity in schools, communities, and at large.	Chicago, IL	https://www.alongwalkhome.org/
As I Plant This Seed, Inc.	Talk to Me mentorship program services middle and high school students, grades 5–12. Groups meet weekly, for ten-week cycles, addressing topics such as self-efficacy, financial literacy, civic responsibility, and more. Community leaders and other accomplished individuals visit to coach the mentees, offering practical application of the week's topic.	Philadelphia, PA	https://asiplantthisseed.com/ IG: asiplantthisseed
Assata's Daughters (AD)	Black woman-led, young person-directed organization rooted in the Black Radical Tradition. Organizes young Black people in Chicago by providing them with political education, leadership development, mentorship, and revolutionary services.	Chicago, IL	https://www.assatasdaughters.org/ IG: assatasdaughtersIG

Audre Lorde Project	Lesbian, gay, bisexual, two-spirit, **trans** and **gender** non-conforming people of color community organization, focusing on the NYC metro area. Through mobilization, education, and capacity-building, we work for community wellness and progressive social and economic **justice.**	Brooklyn, NY	https://alp.org/ IG: audrelordeproject
Brotherhood-Sister Sol	Organization focuses on issues such as leadership development and educational achievement, sexual responsibility, **sexism** and misogyny, political education and social **justice,** Pan-African and Latinx history, and global awareness.	New York, NY	https://brotherhood-sistersol. org/ IG: brosis512
Black Youth Project (BYP) 100	National, member-based organization of Black **activists** and **organizers** (ages 18–35) dedicated to creating **justice** and freedom for all Black people. We build networks focused on transformative leadership development, **direct action** organizing, advocacy, and political education using a **Black queer feminist lens.**	Atlanta, GA; Chicago, IL; Dallas, TX; Washington, DC; Detroit, MI; Durham, NC; Jackson, MS; Milwaukee, WI; New Orleans, LA; New York, NY	https://www.byp100.org/ IG: byp100
Desis Rising and Rising Up (DRUM)	Founded in 2000 to build the **power** of South Asian and Indo-Caribbean low-wage immigrant workers, youth, and families in NYC to win economic and educational **justice,** and civil and immigrant rights.	New York, NY	https://www.drumnyc.org/ IG: drumnyc

Directory of Youth Organizations within the USA

Youth organization	Mission of organization	Location	Social media + website
Detroit Area Youth Uniting Michigan (DAYUM)	Fights for **accountability** from leaders, **justice** for our communities, and a seat at the table for all marginalized youth. An **activist** organization run by high school students. Offers training, **campaign** development, and **direct action**.	Detroit, MI	https://www.facebook.com/Detroit-Area-Youth-Uniting-Michigan-625690124499721/
Detroit Summer	Multiracial, intergenerational collective working to transform communities through youth leadership, creativity, and collective action since 1992. Their Live Arts Media Project (LAMP) is a youth-led response to Detroit's drop-out crisis, which uses music, poetry, and visual art to investigate community problems and generate community-based solutions.	Detroit, MI	https://detroitsummer.wordpress.com/about/ IG: detroit_summer
Girls **Gender** Equity (GGE)	Intergenerational organization committed to the physical, psychological, social, and economic development of girls and women. Through education, organizing and physical fitness, GGE encourages communities to remove barriers and create opportunities for girls and women to live self-determined lives.	New York, NY	https://www.ggenyc.org/ IG: GGENYC
Girls **Justice** League (GJL)	Girls' rights organization dedicated to taking action for social, political, educational, and economic **justice** with and for girls and young women. GJL is a collective of young women and their allies working to build and reinforce a culture where girls are fully empowered and where **gender**, race, and other disparities are identified and confronted in the systems which affect their futures. GJL uses multiple mediums to tell girls' stories, disseminate research that accurately describes girls' current realities and, organize social **justice** toward a different future for all girls.	Philadelphia, PA	http://girlsjusticeleague.org/ IG: girlsjusticephl

GrassROOTS Community Foundation (GCF)	Training organization with emphasis on public health and social action. Supports, develops, and tailors wellness programs for women and girls, particularly those who grew up in economic distress.	Essex, NJ	https:// grassrootscommunityfoundation. org/ IG: grassrootsfound
JUNTOS	Community-led, Latinx immigrant organization in South Philly fighting for our human rights as workers, parents, youth, and immigrants. Believes every human being has the right to a quality education and the freedom to live with dignity regardless of immigration status.	Philadelphia, PA	*https://www.vamosjuntos.org/* IG: vamos_juntos_
Leaders Igniting Transformation (LIT)	Black and Brown-led independent nonprofit organization founded in 2017 to organize young people to build independent political **power** for social, racial, and economic **justice**. Engages in values-based issues and electoral organizing, **direct action,** public policy advocacy, and leadership development.	Milwaukee, WI	https://www.litmke.org/ IG: lit_wi
Make the Road NY and Make the Road Pennsylvania	Make the Road NY integrates four core strategies for concrete change: *Legal and Survival Services* to tackle discrimination, **abuse,** and poverty; *Transformative Education* to develop community members abilities to lead our organization, our **movement,** and society; Community Organizing to transform the systems and **power** structures impacting our communities; and *Policy Innovation* to rewrite unjust rules and make our democracy truly accountable to all of us. Make the Road Pennsylvania is dedicated to organizing the working **class** in Latino communities, building **power** for **justice.**	NY- and PA-wide	https://maketheroadny.org/ https://www.maketheroadpa. org/

Directory of Youth Organizations within the USA

Youth organization	Mission of organization	Location	Social media + website
Next Up	Amplifies the voices and leadership of diverse young people to achieve a more just and equitable Oregon.	OR-wide	https://nextuporegon.org/ IG: nextuporegon
Philadelphia Student Union (PSU)	Builds the **power** of young people to **demand** a high-quality education in the Philadelphia public school system. We are a youth-centered organization and we make positive changes in the short term by learning how to organize to build **power**. We also work toward becoming life-long learners and leaders who can bring diverse groups together to address the problems our communities face.	Philadelphia, PA	*www.phillystudentunion.com* IG: *215studentunion*
Poder in Action	Builds **power** to disrupt and dismantle **systems of oppression** and determine a liberated future as people of color in Arizona.	AZ-wide	https://www.poderinaction.org/ IG: poderinaction
Power U	Organizes and develops the leadership of Black and Brown youth and Black women in South Florida so they may help lead the struggle to liberate all oppressed people.	Miami, FL	https://www.poweru.org/ IG: poweru305
Project South	Youth development work laying foundation for youth-led organizing to address the most pressing concerns in public schools and in Atlanta's communities of color. Its annual summer program, the Septima Clark Community Power Institute, trains up to forty predominantly Black youth to become more effective **organizers**, facilitators, and leaders in the community.	Atlanta, GA	https://projectsouth.org/

Providence Student Union (PSU)	Builds student **power** to improve education and well-being. Envisions a true "union for students" that increases young people's collective **power** and ensures our frustrations, **demands**, and dreams are heard.	Providence, RI	https://www.pvdstudentunion.org/ IG: pvdstudentunion
Radical Monarchs	Creates opportunities for young girls of color to form fierce sisterhood, celebrate their identities, and contribute radically to their communities.	Oakland, CA	https://radicalmonarchs.org/ IG: radicalmonarchs
Sadie Nash Leadership Project	Strengthens, empowers, and equips young women and **gender-expansive** youth of color as agents for change in their lives and in the world. Operating at the intersections of love and rigor, we use the methodology of popular education to build community, critical consciousness, and college and career readiness.	NY/NJ-wide	http://www.sadienash.org/ IG: sadienashleadershipproject
Social **Justice** Leadership Institute (SJLI)	American Friends Service Committee (AFSC) program focused on developing youth leadership through intensive social **justice** training. Brings together young people (ages 14–18) for training around personal/emotional development, **campaign** development, historical context of social issues, critical thinking and analysis of **oppression**, and leadership development.	Philadelphia, PA	https://www.afsc.org/sjli
UPROSE	Intergenerational, multiracial, nationally recognized community organization promoting sustainability and resiliency in Brooklyn's Sunset Park neighborhood through **community organizing**, education, Indigenous and youth leadership development, and cultural/artistic expression.	Brooklyn, NY	https://www.uprose.org/ IG: uprosebrooklyn

Directory of Youth Organizations within the USA

Youth organization	Mission of organization	Location	Social media + website
Viet Lead	Grassroots community organization creating a vision and **strategy** for community self-determination, social **justice**, and cultural resilience.	Philadelphia, PA and South Jersey, NJ	https://www.vietlead.org/
W.E. Reign	Our mission is to create safe-brave spaces where young people who identify as Black and girl are visible, and their strengths, needs, voices, and stories are centered as they define themselves, practice living unapologetically, and develop the skills needed to become change agents in their own lives and communities.	Philadelphia, PA	http://wereign.net/ IG: we.reign
Young Women's Freedom Center (YWFC)	Founded in 1993 to empower and inspire cis and **trans** young women, **trans** young men, and **gender-expansive** young people in California who have been disproportionately impacted by incarceration, racist and sexist policies, the juvenile and criminal **justice** systems, and/or the underground street economy, to create positive change in their lives and communities.	CA–wide	https://www.youngwomenfree.org/ IG: young_women_free
Youth Arts and Self-Expression Project (YASP)	Youth-led **movement** to end the practice of incarcerating young people as adults and create a world without youth incarceration. Young people who have been through the adult court system are at the forefront, leading the **movement** to keep young people out of prisons and to create new possibilities for youth around the city. Through work in Philadelphia jails, provides spaces for incarcerated young people to express themselves creatively and to develop as leaders both within and beyond the prison walls.	Philadelphia, PA	*http://www.yasproject.com/* IG: *yasprojectphilly*

Youth **Justice** Coalition	Working to build a youth, family, and formerly and currently incarcerated people's **movement** to challenge America's addiction to incarceration and race, **gender** and **class** discrimination in Los Angeles County's, California's and the nation's juvenile and criminal injustice systems.	Inglewood, CA	https://youthjusticela.org/
Youth United for Change (YUC)	Provides young leaders in Philadelphia with a critical political, historical, and economic understanding of society, and to empower them to improve the quality of their lives and communities.	Philadelphia, PA	www.youthunitedforchange.org IG: YUCphilly

IV. Resources for Turnt Up for Radical Joy

Before starting any community builder, especially one that is asking for folks to be a bit more vulnerable, it's important to develop some clear **boundaries** for how you all want to engage each other. Creating agreements gives you that opportunity.

Creating Agreements

Creating agreements as a group is an important way to create what becomes normal in the space or what becomes the culture for the work to happen. Agreements help set clear **boundaries**, so folks can be clear in how they interact with respect and dignity. They also help give people tools to step into their healing in a group setting. These should be written out and be in a very visible space when you meet so that anyone can refer to them when someone makes a mistake or goes against an agreement. Here is a list of sample commitments:

One mic (allow for one person at a time to speak).

Take space, make space (be responsible in how much or how little you are contributing to the conversation and challenge when you are becoming too comfortable).

Don't yuck my yum (don't belittle someone else's excitement about something if you don't agree with it).

Use "I" statements (speak from your own experience).

Save the story, share the lesson (similar to "what is said here, stays here"; this acknowledges you might want to share the lesson of what someone is sharing, but leave out the details to respect their **boundaries**).

Mind

Community Builders that Nourish the Mind	How to Play
Chant making	Throughout history, creating and using a chant during protests has been a powerful way to keep the energy up! These are short sentences that have a rhythm and are usually done as a "call and response." This means a chant leader will say one part of the chant and the rest of the people will repeat or respond to what they said. You might be more familiar with chants as a practice of Buddhism or cheerleaders. In all these instances, chants are a way to tap into the **power** of your spirit to move people. You can create a chant to add to the identity of your group. One way we would end meetings or actions [in TUFF Girls] was the way many Black radical groups have ended their meetings or actions: by chanting the Assata Shakur quote. We would say it three times; first as a whisper, then in an even tone, and then as a roar: "It is our duty to fight for our freedom, it's our duty to win, we must love and support each other, we have nothing to lose but our chains." Chants at an action should not only sound good, but also name what you want, helping to increase the energy and pressure toward making it a reality. The value of this became crystal clear to me during an action in Cleveland, OH, where I was working with hundreds of people to de-arrest a child and bring him to his mother's custody. People hooked arms in a circle around the cop cars and chanted Assata's line, "We have nothing to lose but our chains," for over thirty minutes. He was eventually freed into his mother's arms.

Here are a couple of popular chants you can hear at actions:

Call: "What do we want?
Response: "**Justice!**"
Call: "When we do we want it?"
Response: "Now!"

Call: "Show me what a **feminist** looks like!
Response: "This is what a **feminist** looks like!"

Now, go to YouTube and type in "Black Youth Project 100 chants" for more inspiration.

Name games

Name games are really helpful when you are bringing new people together. One simple name game is to have participants sit in a circle where you ask everyone to think about an adjective that starts with the first letter of their name and describes them. For example, I would be "Energetic E." The challenge then is to have one person introduce themselves with their adjective, and then the person to the right of them to introduce themselves as well as the person who just went. Then, the person to the right of them introduces themselves and the two people who went before. This continues until the last person has to introduce everyone in the group. This is often very hard! You can give that person a break by opening it up to anyone in the group to see if they can take on the challenge.

Silent DJ

Perhaps you want people to remember certain words or phrases. In TUFF Girls, we wanted folks to remember the **principles**. In this fun guessing game, you can break people into pairs or do this as a whole group. One person has headphones and music on, and the other person or group of people are saying a word or phrase that the person listening to music is trying to guess based on how they are reading the other person/people's lips.

Group poem

Spread out into a circle and share that you will all create a group poem, line by line, with no paper. Take a prompt and have them finish the sentence and pass it to the next person in the circle until everyone has gone. Prompts can be: "If you knew me, you would know . . ." or "I am from . . . ." Go through at least 2–3 rounds of the prompt so that folks can work on going deeper in their response. For example, I have seen people be very literal in round one of "I am from . . ." and simply share their neighborhood, address, or city. Then in their second round, I heard them say, "I am from the strength and courage of my big sister."

Letter writing

With all the technology and social media available to us, we have moved away from writing letters. What makes a letter special is that it holds the unique handwriting of a person and can be kept forever. You can write letters to your future self, or letters to each other when you want to encourage gratitude or communication. You might also notice that many people in your group have loved ones in prison whose absence impacts them. Creating space and time to encourage folks to write letters to their loved ones can be a healing way to express themselves and feel connected to their loved ones. It can be harder to get started on those letters on your own. Doing this in a group can make it fun and motivating.

"Move your seat"   For this you will need a chair for each person, except for the person in the middle. That person is trying to get into the seat in the circle. They do this by saying, "Move your seat if . . ." and then filling that sentence with something true about themselves. This could be something like: "if you were born in January" or "if you have been in love." For the people who also find this statement to be true for them, they must find a new seat before the person in the middle or anyone else takes all the seats. Whoever cannot find a seat then stands in the middle and repeats the prompt. If you are leading this game, you may encourage people to get a little deeper if you find they are sticking to safe options like colors or what they are wearing. This is a community builder that invites folks to be a little more vulnerable. This is challenging, but the reward is also knowing you are rarely if ever alone in a truth that you have.

Body

Community Builders that Nourish the Body	How to Play
Mirror movement	Choose a playlist that is fun and upbeat, but not too fast. Form a circle with the group of people you are with. Explain that one person will give a dance movement for thirty seconds, and the group will mirror their movement. They then pass it to the person to the left or right until the entire circle has gone. Similar to the previous activity, people who feel shy about dancing or who have been teased for their dancing might not like this activity. Remember, the goal isn't to perform the best dance moves; it is to help people feel free enough in their bodies to move in ways that feel good to them. Don't forget to debrief and remind people about the goal.
Nature walks	Taking a group walk in nature or at a park can offer a lot of collective healing. Being in nature encourages the body to do deeper breathing which nourishes our lungs and our nervous systems. If you live in an inner city, you might have to do some research to see where there is a park or hiking trail and figure out how to get there with the help of an adult.
Cooking	We all need to eat. It's a basic human need. Even if you don't know how to cook, you can always pull a recipe from online and divide the work. This requires some adult assistance if you have to work with knives in order to cut or if you need a kitchen and other appliances, but making food like snacks doesn't always require that. Be creative.

Facials

Most of the ingredients for a facial are right in your kitchen or in the supermarket. Making a facial can help exfoliate the skin (take away dead skin cells) or hydrate it. You just have to be aware that everyone has a different skin type. For people who have sensitive or dry skin, you can blend oatmeal, olive oil, and honey. For someone who has more oily skin, you can blend cucumber and rosemary in a blender and then add salt. Once you have made your facials, you can pair up, wash each other's face with the face wash you normally use, dry the skin, and then gently apply the mask you made. Let it sit for 15 minutes then rinse. Use toner or witch hazel to wipe off any residue that stays behind. Hydrate each other's skin with face cream. This is a really nice bonding activity of tender touch and **consent** that can leave you feeling more connected to another person and with smoother skin!

Shake down, countdown

This is a nice activity to do when people need an energy boost. Ask people to stand up and demonstrate it for them. Explain that you are going to countdown from 10 to 1, each time you shake your left hand, then your right, your hips, your left leg, and then your right leg. Tell them that the goal is to count in unison and increase the energy in the room. Demonstrate by shaking your right hand as you say loudly, "10-9-8-7-6-5-4-3-2-1," and then shake the left hand and say the same, and repeat for the hips, and legs. Start again, but this time, start from 9 and count down to 1 for each hand/hip/leg. Once you finish, start at 8 and continue this until you count all the way down to 1. By the time you reach 5, there is often a strong rhythm in how the group is counting collectively. And by the time you get to 1, the energy is very high, and people usually end up clapping and cheering. A few folks may still feel confused when you first explain the instructions but assure them that as long as a few people get it, once the group gets started it will make sense.

Block cleanup	Sometimes the best community builder for your group is the one where you are directly helping the community around you. Everyone loves walking in a neighborhood that is clean. Often, in neighborhoods in large cities where there is food insecurity, there also aren't a lot of trash cans. If there are trash cans, the city may not dispose of this trash regularly so it can pile up. A block cleanup in these neighborhoods is a powerful way to say that despite the city not caring about who lives there, your group does.

Spirit

Community Builders that Nourish the Spirit	How to Honor
Vision board	A vision board is a collage of images and words you gather that represent experiences you want to call into your life. You can cut these from magazines or newspapers, or print them out from the Internet. It is based on the idea that if you keep these images in a place where you can meditate on them daily, that you can become more motivated to embody them or take more action towards experiencing them. TUFF Girls made a vision board for the organization, including words and phrases like "soul," "protect," "leadership training," and "**activist** of the family." We had images of Black women protesting, smiling, and resting together.

Libations to the ancestors

This is a very sacred tradition of African people and should be treated as such. Pouring libations to honor the **ancestors**, or people who have died, has survived colonialism and slavery. You might see family members pour out liquor on the ground to honor people they have lost. This is a form of pouring libation. If you are outside, then you can pour water into the grass as you call each name. If you are inside, then you can find a plant and pour a little water as you call each name. Start first by grounding everyone in the space by taking a breath. The facilitator should then explain that when we call out the names of our **ancestors**, we can honor their presence and their wisdom, and bring this into the room. First, the facilitator should give a land acknowledgment by honoring the **ancestors** who were the original people of the land. You can find which Indigenous community/communities is/ are native to where you live by a simple Google search. Since this is an African tradition, you would then honor the Africans brought to this country whose sacrifices we stand upon. Then, you would open it up for people to name people in their family or lineage who they want to lift up, followed by other people in history who they want to lift up. After each name, the leader pours water and says, "*ashe*," the Yoruba word which affirms. It has various meanings, one of them being, "the universe says yes." Once you have completed all names, you can close by saying ashe three times.

Appreciation circle	Sitting in a circle, the leader starts by turning to the person on their left (because the heart is on the left side of the body). The leader says: "I see you [name of the person], and I appreciate you for . . . ." They then turn to the person to the left and continue this until the entire circle has been appreciated.
Let it burn, let it go	This is a great exercise for the spirit if there is a lot of built-up tension or you are looking to deepen the sense of connection between people in a group. You can remind people that the element of fire is a powerful cleanser. In fact, sequoia trees, which can be found in California, need the heat of fire in order to reproduce. Invite the group to consider what they want to release, perhaps a tension, an old beef, something nasty someone told them, etc. Caution them against choosing something very traumatic as you may not have the ability to help them close what may feel like an open wound. If their spirit feels ready, they can then write this out, and together you can burn these papers. This burning activity should only be done outside, in a fire pit or a pot with water nearby to be done safely. Explain that the experience doesn't change, but the weight of it on their spirit can decrease by releasing it to the fire.

GLOSSARY

*Note: Words with * were adapted from the SOUL curriculum on Youth Organizing. Words with ** were adapted from* Fumbling Towards Repair *by Mariame Kaba and Shira Hassan.*

Abolition: Commitment to not engage in any practice that dehumanizes and punishes others even as we keep people safe and respond to violence. It is a vision and **strategy** for responding to **harm** without police and prisons or trying to be like them.

Abuse: Any action that intentionally **harms** another person. This includes physical, emotional, spiritual, financial, and sexual abuse. For children this also includes neglecting the basic needs of children (housing, food, education/schooling, **protection** from exploitation such as child trafficking/illegal/forced work).

Accountability****:** Willingness to accept responsibility for one's harmful actions or behaviors.

Activist/s: A person—or a group of people—who takes some kind of action towards an injustice.

Agency: The **power** you have to make choices in a situation.

Agenda: The goal of a meeting and the list of items you will discuss to meet that goal.

Ally: A person who is not directly impacted or affected by an injustice but is willing to struggle with people who are.

Ancestors: Persons who have died/left their physical body and now exist in the spiritual realm. Enlightened ancestors are those who are healed enough to be able to provide you guidance when you call them for support or **protection**.

Anti-Blackness: Racist beliefs and practices that specifically target Black people and anything that is associated or connected to Black people/Blackness.

Anxiety: An intense, constant, and overwhelming worry of places, people, and/or everyday interactions.

BIPOC: Black, Indigenous, people of color.

Black feminist/s: Believe in self-critique and a politics of care and **accountability**, and that liberating Black women will lead to the freedom of others. "Black feminism" was coined by Barbara Smith and others in the Combahee River Collective Statement of 1974. After this, it became a theoretical framework and organizing **strategy** for liberating Black women from racial, **gender**, sexual, and **class oppression**. The work of TUFF Girls was Black feminism in practice, even if we didn't always call it that by name.

Black queer feminist lens: Think of the lenses of a pair of reading glasses: it's what helps a person see what's in front of them more clearly. The Black queer feminist lens seeks to center the experiences of the most marginalized person of a marginalized group, building on the legacy of Black feminism and Black trans leadership.

Boundaries: Personal limits or rules that you have for how you want other people to treat you.

Campaign*: An intensive, sustained, and coordinated organizing fight that uses collective **power** of organizations to strike at a **target** until it meets your **demands**. They seek to redistribute **power**/or resources, bring institutional change, and build grassroots leaders.

Capitalism: System of making money where workers do not have any **power** in how or what they create. Within capitalism, owners make money and profit at the expense of workers and the health of the community/environment.

Caste system: Started in India over 3,000 years ago, it is a system where people are placed into different groups before they are born that determine what jobs they can take and who they can marry. "Caste hierarchy" is the fact that some caste members are given more **privileges** than others. Some castes experience discrimination or even violence for simply existing.

Cisgender: A **gender** identity where your body parts match the **gender** assigned to you as birth by a doctor.

Civic engagement: Addressing an issue of public concern by engaging government or civic associations. This may look like testifying at a school board or city council, supporting the voting process, creating and signing petitions, or exercising your First Amendment right to protest a public issue.

Class: Social status based on how much money your household makes or has been able to save over generations. Since children are not expected to make money to earn a living on their own, their class status matches the class status of their parent/caregiver.

Classism: A system of power that benefits rich people at the expense of the working class and people who are cash poor.

Class privilege: Unearned advantages that come with being born into a middle-**class** or wealthy family.

Class struggle: Within a system of **capitalism**, the class struggle is the tension between the capitalist **class** who are exploiting workers in order to produce more profits, and the working **class**, who are resisting their exploitation by organizing.

Climate change: Also known as the "climate crisis," referring to the extreme and odd weather conditions created by corporations that build pipelines in the ground, use major machinery on large farms that release carbon meant to remain in the ground, and other actions against the physical environment. Often these are done to increase how much money corporations/developers make.

Colonization: The process of one group of people using their **power** and resources to take over the land and resources of another group of people. Usually done by violent means, the people colonized are also forced to give up their culture and beliefs.

Community organizing: The process of groups of people identifying an injustice or a problem in the community and motivating others to take strategic action while transforming the relations of **power**. Mutual aid organizing, campaigns with clear **targets**

and **demands**, political education, and cultural work are different kinds of community organizing.

Consent: The permission someone grants you that is verbal and nonverbal. Consent can change from moment to moment.

Container: An intentional way to create a space with people where you are fully present and able to listen to as they share and process certain experiences.

Decolonize: The active process of unlearning beliefs and attitudes that support the **power dynamics** of **colonization**; the active process of dismantling systems of **power** that serves the larger project of **imperialism, capitalism, white supremacy**, and **patriarchy**.

Demand/s: A very clear ask of what you want in order to address an injustice.

Direct action: Action or tactic that is engaged to increase public pressure in order to meet a **demand** from a **target**. This might look like collectively walking out of your classroom and holding a rally in the lunchroom to get more **BIPOC** authors into the school curriculum.

Directly impacted: The people who are most affected by an injustice you are working on.

Disability justice: The work of **activists** who center the needs and realities of people who are differently abled (physically, mentally, and emotionally), while also recognizing other oppressed identities they may have. For example, students of color with disabilities have higher suspension rates than students of color, who also have higher suspension rates than their white counterparts. Disability justice would get at the root of why that happens in a way that centers the unique experiences of students of color with disabilities.

Ego: The voice inside your head that sees yourself based on how the world sees you. For example, a "perfectionist," someone who appears to be concerned with always being perfect, may have a wounded ego.

Fake tough: It's feeling good and even powerful about bullying or harming someone just because you can. This behavior helps to feed systems of **power** like **anti-Blackness**, **patriarchy**, **transphobia**, and **capitalism**. This is a red flag for a person aligning themselves with oppressors and/or not addressing past/existing **trauma**.

Femme/s: A person who highly identifies with femininity or being a girl or woman.

Feminist: A person who works towards understanding the impact of **patriarchy** and transforms patriarchal systems. There are several waves and branches of feminism.

Food justice: A **movement** working to protect the right of all communities to afford access to nutritious and food common to their culture, while advocating for people who play a role in the food production process. This includes farmers and all those who produce, package, distribute, and deliver food to supermarkets, restaurants, and farmer's markets. This is a global **movement** that has historically been led by **BIPOC** workers of the food industry. It works closely with those in the environmental **justice movement** and on the fight for sustainable energy.

Food racism/food apartheid: The historical and negative impact where **BIPOC** neighborhoods don't have access to affordable whole foods, while also having overexposure to a lot of fast food restaurants and low-quality food stores in those same areas.

Freedom parties: A community organizing tool that invites a group of people to party with a clear purpose: to raise awareness of social injustices in order to build solidarity towards collective action.

Gender binary: The idea that there are only two **genders**: female (girl/woman) AND/OR male (boy/man).

Genocide: The process of exterminating a group of people over time. According to the Genocide Convention of 1948, this includes the killing of members of a group, causing serious bodily or psychological **harm** on a group, intentionally inflicting on the living conditions of a group such that it will lead to total or part devastation of that group, imposing practices and policies that would prevent births from happening in the group, and forcing children of one group to stay with another group.

Gender: Gender is how someone sees themselves in the body they are in. It is a social construct meaning that it can vary from society to society, change over time, and is learned in the social interactions of an environment.

Gender expression: The various ways that an individual decides to present their **gender** through behavior, mannerisms, clothing, hair, and other adornments (shoes, jewelry, makeup, nails, etc.). They might be feminine, masculine, androgynous, and/or fluid.

Gender expansive: When a person identifies with a **gender** outside of the **gender binary**. This includes people who are **trans, nonbinary**, and intersex.

Generational trauma: The psychological effects of **trauma** from previous generations that gets carried into the next generation.

Harm/s: A negative impact on a person's mind/body/spirit. Harm can be caused intentionally or not.

Healer: Healing happens in community, but it also takes a person taking initiative in tending to their wounds to know what they need from themselves and community. **Healer of self** also recognizes the medicine everyone holds within and can share through practices of care, compassion, curiosity, and connection.

Healing: The lifelong process of becoming whole; growth after **trauma**. Healing is the slow, messy process of feeling through the feelings associated with **harm** with intentional care in order to step back into your full **power**.

Heterosexism: System of inequality where heterosexual people have **privileges** at the expense of the **LGBTQIA** community.

Homophobia: Irrational fear of and intentional **prejudice**/violence towards people who are gay, lesbian, queer, or questioning.

Housing justice: The fight to address root causes of why people are houseless or live in unsafe conditions and to increase access to safe, affordable housing. Additionally, this **movement** confronts the historical and ongoing housing disparity caused by **racism** in order to create more equitable and sustainable housing solutions.

Imperialism*: Global economic, political, and social system wherein so-called "First World" nations control "Third World" nations to gain **power** and profit from their labor, markets, and natural resources.

Indigenous people: Indigenous with a capital I refers to First Nation groups such as the Cherokee and Blackfoot people. You probably have heard them referred to as Native Americans, but this title doesn't honor that they lived on the land before European colonizers named it "America." The term "indigenous," in general, refers to the original people of a place or something being original to a region of the world.

Inner child: The part of each person that represents their younger self and able to be curious, innocent, playful, joyful, and in awe of something. It may also hold wounds from early childhood **trauma**.

Institution: An organization of people that is supposed to provide support for the needs of society. Examples include schools, hospitals, places of employment, etc.

Institutional oppression: Policies and practices that are embedded in systems (education, criminal **justice**, employment, housing authorities, etc.) that serve to keep certain people in control of others (e.g., police violence, job discrimination, housing districts, etc.).

Internalized oppression: Taking the beliefs of others and applying that thinking to your own experience. For example, judging your own skin color, or hair texture, and deciding that one kind is better than another within the race or ethnic group.

Interpersonal oppression: Idea that one group is better than another and therefore has the right to control the other. (For example: when someone tells you, "you are smart for a Black girl"; or, white people crossing to the other side of the street to avoid being on the side a Black person is on.)

Intersectionality: Systems of oppression overlap to create unique experiences for people with multiple identity categories. This term was coined by Kimberlé Williams Crenshaw to discuss the unique experiences of Black women who experience both **racism** and **sexism** at the same time.

Justice: There are many different definitions of justice according to one's history and culture. The United States' justice system is based on a definition of justice that equals it to punishment in the form of loss of mobility, cash payment/restitution, and/or prison time. Restorative and **transformative justice** are other definitions and frameworks for defining justice through either restoring relationships through dialogue, and/or transforming the root cause of **harm** through a community **accountability** process. This includes recognition of **harm** done; having resources to begin our **healing** path; putting in place resources to prevent more **harm** in the future.

Land justice: The fight to address the ability of people who have been historically oppressed through slavery and **colonization** (i.e., Black and **Indigenous people**) to have access to land ownership.

LGBTQIA: Lesbian, gay, bisexual, **trans,** queer, intersex, and asexual.

#MeToo movement: Movement in the mid-2010s that started on social media and that used the stories of survivors of sexual assault to cause international pressure to end **rape culture.**

Movement*: Large-scale, sustained mobilization of masses of individuals and organizations united in common action by a common issue or vision. Movements are bigger than any single organization's efforts, although organizations are key to developing sustainable and effective movements.

Neuroplasticity: The brain's ability to heal neural pathways from physical **trauma** through different activities that utilize encounters with new experiences and environments, as well various treatment plans that are focused on processing and integrating **trauma** in the body and building new neural pathways in the brain.

Nonbinary: Gender identity where a person does not identify as a girl/woman or boy/man.

Oppression: Combination of **prejudice, privilege,** and institutional **power** that benefits some people while harming others.

Organizer/s: Person who works with groups of people, including organizations, to make **demands** for **justice** and get people's needs met. An organizer is also building up the leadership of themselves and others through political education, discussion, and collective action.

Patriarchy: The political, social, and cultural belief system that narrowly defines masculinity as domination and organizes **gender** on a social ladder that places cis boys and men at the top, and **femmes**/girls/women and **trans** boys and men at the bottom.

Power/power dynamics: There are many definitions of power, some which contradict each other. Most definitions of power in the US define it in terms of domination, or a relationship where someone or something has the ability to have influence over something or oppress it. Systems of power such as the ones listed on pages 34–36 are great examples of how it reflects unequal and oppressive relationships. Many Black and Indigenous **feminists** help us restore our original definition of power that was about relationships of connection, with self, with others, and with the land.

Prejudice: The everyday personal judgments that someone makes of a group of people based on their own ill-informed and negative understanding they associate with that group. This kind of **harm** usually happens on an interpersonal level.

Principle/s: It is a position you take that reflects how you intend to show up in the world.

Privilege/s: Unearned advantage that a person receives based on their identity (e.g., **class privilege**, male privilege, white privilege, heterosexual privilege, **cisgender** privilege, etc.).

Protector: One who helps keep themselves and others safe and stands up for people who are victims of injustice.

Racism: System of inequality where white people have more **privileges** and advantages than—and these are at the expense of—**BIPOC** communities.

Radical healing: Building caring relationships, and nurturing healthy relationships with Black and Brown youth, and helping them build a political consciousness about community issues that motivate them to confront neighborhood problems.

Radical joy: The intentional practice of cultivating joy and pleasure, as we tend to (re-)do the harms and impacts of supremacy and inequity.

Rape culture: Beliefs and practices that make sexual **harm** appear normal.

Redlining: The practice of the real estate market to draw red lines on maps around neighborhoods where Black people lived so that the banks would not give those families loans when they tried to take one out for a home in another area. The redlining of the 1930s and 1970s also meant that these neighborhoods had less value and received less investments from the government, which has had an impact to this day.

Resources: Materials, money, or people that make things run smoothly. For example, a school with many resources may have things like smart boards, a laptop for each student, updated science labs, a state-of-the-art gym, etc.

Restorative justice (RJ): A process of making things right when one person has caused **harm** to another.

Scholar-activist and Scholar-Activism: A person who dedicates their reading, writing, and research to addressing injustices and creating solutions.

School-to-prison pipeline: The process of pushing students, typically Black and Brown students, out of school and into prison. This happens when there is increased police presence, a decrease in counselors, overcrowded schools with limited **resources**, and other practices that emphasize order over education.

Self-talk: The internal conversation you have with yourself about yourself. Negative self-talk usually is very unforgiving, judgmental, critical, mean, and self-hating. Positive self-talk usually is curious, compassionate, honest, gentle, and respectful. In each case, we can find ourselves repeating comments others have made about us. Our work is to become our most honest and loving selves and talk to ourselves from that place.

Sex: There are many definitions of the word sex. One definition refers to the physical aspects of your body and biology to assign a **gender** category, as well as the physical aspects your body transitions into as a person discovers and embraces their **gender**. The second definition refers to the physical activities that promote sexual arousal between two consenting adults or two consenting minors.

Sexism: The system of inequality where cis men have more **privilege** at the expense of cis women, **trans** folks, and people who are **nonbinary**.

Sexuality: This refers to how a person understands and defines their sexual or intimate desires, or how they describe their sexual orientation. For example, they might identify as queer, asexual, bisexual, heterosexual, monogamous, or polyamorous.

Strategy: Plan of action for getting a **target** to meet a **demand**.

Street harassment: The unwanted attention that a person gets while in public that includes being whistled or yelled at, followed, groped or grabbed, or talked to in a sexual or violent way.

Study: The practice of reading, writing, and thinking in order to better understand something.

Systems of oppression: The processes, policies, institutions, and cultural practices that work together to benefit one group of people over another.

Target: This term has different definitions depending on the context. In the context of **organizing** (as it is mostly used here) it refers to a person in a position of **power** that needs to be moved in order to meet the **demands** of an organized **strategy**.

Transatlantic slave trade: The European theft and trading of African people during the 1600s–1800s that forced millions of Africans into the Americas, the Caribbean, and Europe in order to provide free labor (e.g., farming, cooking, building homes and equipment, raising the children of slaveholders, making clothes, etc.)

Transformative justice (TJ): An approach to conflict, **harm**, and violence that does not rely on the police or prisons. It addresses root causes of **harm** while centering the **healing** of the survivor as well as the person who caused **harm**. Through a process of dialogue and education, it offers steps and **resources** to prevent violence from happening again and to transform **systems of oppression**.

Trans/transgender: A person whose **gender** does not match their **sex** assigned at birth.

Transphobia: The fear and hatred of, and **prejudice** towards, people who identify as **transgender**.

Trauma/s: There are many different kinds of trauma that affect us as an individual and as a people. Individual trauma is the negative impact on our mental/physical/emotional/spiritual health due to an event or series of events in one's lifetime. **Generational trauma** refers to the impact of negative historical events on a generation of people that gets passed down to the next generation.

White supremacy: The belief that whiteness represents all that is right, true, and beautiful and is the standard for all humanity.

FOR THE ADULT WHO BOUGHT THIS BOOK FOR THEIR YOUNG PERSON

From the depths of my heart, I appreciate you. Thank you for believing and supporting our youth during what may be their toughest stage of growth yet. For starting the courageous conversations you wish you had at their age. For helping them name the violence of the system on their bodies and on their imaginations. For all your care work, seen and unseen. For pouring into them when they feel distant and hard to understand. Your perseverance literally shapes our future. I hope this book helps to shoulder this sacred labor of yours, and helps water what you have seeded, or helps to seed soil you have watered.

At a time when state governments are banning books and curriculums about the past and current **harms** of this country's history, as well as the organizing and resistance Black and **LGBTQIA** communities have done in the face of these **harms**, and introduces dangerous anti-**trans** legislation, this book is emerging in a moment when young people need more material to archive this history and our resistance. The Center for Disease Control and Prevention (CDC) recently announced a mental health crisis with teen girls. This book is a reminder for these teens, and for you, why that is, and what we can all do to create better conditions for teen girls to thrive in, especially if they are **trans**.

If you don't identify as a Black or Brown girl, you might already understand that you are in a relationship with a young person who is often the most invisibilized and hypervisibilized person in the room. Thank you for being a witness and an advocate. For doing the work to hold yourself as you hold yourself accountable. For all the studying and questioning of her material conditions, and all the **healing** and unlearning to access a more radical **agency** that extracts **white supremacy** within and nourishes Black **power**. I hope your **privileges** are leveraged to disarm her oppressor, the one within and the ones you know.

If you do identify as a Black or Brown girl, I hope this book allows your **inner child** to feel seen and inspired by the process of creating new intergenerational stories about toughening up for our individual and collective survival. Like you, I learned early how unfair and unkind the world can be. We didn't just mature more quickly than the boys because of textbook biology, girls had bodies which they did not own. Often, our families, trusted adults, and strangers held us to higher standards with less mercy than our cis, masculine, and white counterparts. We were policed or punished out of nostalgia or fear or sick fantasies of Black girlhood. We were given more caretaking responsibilities that taught us to put other people's needs before our own and wear our self-abandonment with a badge of honor.

We were fed mixed messages about safety and pleasure, where the line between good and bad girls was thin and made no space for the gray. Bad girls were not worthy of support or **protection** because, well, they were bad. We were told to be good by pushing through, thickening our skin, and that being twice as good as the white kids was a requirement for success.

*What did your pushing through look like as a kid?
What did it teach you about your power as a young
person?*

For me, pushing through was masking insecurities
by overachieving, people pleasing, and bottling up a
whole lot inside. Not only did this make me vulnerable to more **trauma** as I got older, but it also kept me
isolated from the support systems within and around
me. As you read in Chapter 2, intentional **healing**
wouldn't start until I was well into my twenties.

When I started TUFF Girls in 2014, it was out of
a deep urge from my gut to create a space for Black
and Brown girls to reimagine pushing through and to
build an intergenerational support system. For over
five years we had a lot of transformative moments in
TUFF Girls, made lots of mistakes, and created some
really powerful relationships with each other and more
significantly, with ourselves. And in its seventh year,
in the spirit of reimagining what it means to "push
through," we decided to sunset the organization.

As we bring TUFF Girls to a close and as I reflect
on my years of working with young people and their
villages, this book is a place for those learnings to
rematriate, as some Indigenous **feminists** would say.[1]
Similar to the Akan symbol of *sankofa*, rematriation
is a return to the origin of something for growth.
This book is a set of notes for loud and quiet girls
rediscovering and channeling their innate **power**, the
kind they came into this world embodying before
our systems and adult fears/fantasies retooled them.
I hope this book inspires what our freedom-fighting
ancestors always hoped for their descendants: to go

---

[1] See, for one example, Lee Maracle, *I Am Woman: A Native
Perspective on Sociology and Feminism* (Vancouver: Press Gang
Publishers, 2002).

inward and toward each other as they make sense of injustice. Help them name the **harms** of **racism, classism, sexism, transphobia,** and **imperialism** so that they can **decolonize** their mind, hearts, and spirits and rematriate towards a path of dignity and self-determination.

For most people, actualizing this process of restoring **power** is our life lesson, not something we achieve by the time we graduate high school. (Me! I am most people.) No one has all the answers for how we dismantle **oppression,** or how we engage and learn from young people in that process. It will take continued experimenting, and as my friend Stephanie says, a process of "failing up." This book is an invitation to keep our eyes focused on liberation and a reminder that we don't have to—nor is it sustainable—to simply push through. We can create buoys within ourselves and with each other, in order to rise above oppressive waters and travel towards our North Star of collective liberation. I hope the stories, questions, and activities in this book offer you the tools to make those buoys with your young folks.

The history of the world has shown us different kinds of intergenerational relationship-building projects and consciousness-raising exercises that have birthed the kind of global mass **movement** building required for **justice** and safety. Whether it was the general strike of enslaved Africans that Northern abolitionists leveraged to win the US Civil War; the children's marches of the American civil rights **movement**; the decolonial struggles of African independence of the 1960s; the Chicano and Puerto Rican Independence **movements**; the American Indian **movement**; the Cultural Revolution of China, the Black Power **movement** in the US; the Dalit-led resistance of the late 1960s and 1970s in India; or, the **movement** against apartheid in South Africa and Palestine (both of which had been ongoing for decades and had peak moments in the late 1980s and 1990s). Up to this day, Palestine still fights to end one of the longest military occupations from its Israeli colonizers. Through it all, young people were and continue to always be there, and have been some of the greatest victims and victors in the frontline of these struggles. For those who did not and do not join in the struggle, as political prisoner Mumia Abul-Jamal would say, "If this is the lost generation, then we must find them."[2]

How do we continue to answer the call of history now, and work with young people to refuse our collective **oppression**? Responding to the Trump administration's call for brute force that stood on the shoulders of liberal Democrat war-mongering empire, more recent land-based struggles for housing security and food sovereignty, **climate change**, immigration reforms, and **protection** of rights of those who are Muslim, **trans**, and disabled, have created a new united front.

One might say we are in the heart of the Age of Aquarius, which is to say, we are in the flow of a broken dam ushering in a new world. Many of us are awakening, as we name a thing a thing, starting with how systemic **oppression** has been the root of our ancestral **trauma** or the reason why we play small, or why we as a culture tend to focus solely on the individual. It is why we struggle to believe that change is possible and the reason for why it was so hard to love ourselves. Trump's presidency revealed just how much of this country is loyal to a racist and sexist social order, and the global pandemic of COVID-19 showed how deadly that order continues to be for

<hr>

[2] Mumia Abu Jamal, *Live from Death Row* (New York: First Avon Books, 1996).

Black and Brown people. Many, young and old, are still unwilling to see particularly Black people as full human beings, let alone people who deserve dignity and freedom.

Perhaps, however, the greatest victory of this moment has been the popular uprising of 2020, sparked by the police killing of George Floyd. The mass outrage of people across age, race, **gender**, and **class** helped to skyrocket the efforts of the abolitionist **movement** into the mainstream national media, city councils, and even Congress. After decades of this **movement** being seen as *too radical* for advocating for a divest-invest **strategy** that moves funds from police and prisons towards education, **healing**, housing and employment **resources**, more and more people have finally been inspired to question: can the culture of policing actually keep communities safe or does it cause more **harm**? If it does cause more **harm**, and like so many others I believe that it does, not only must we defund the police but we must also abolish the police in our minds and hearts.

I have worked in schools where there were no uniformed police, but there were cops sitting behind the teacher's desk. Regrettably, in certain moments, that cop was me. This book is about the questions and meditations we all need to sit with to better build our emotional infrastructure for sharing **power** with youth as we also guide them and be guided. Ultimately, this means that this is a book about **abolition**, and the politics of care and skill-building it requires from us all.

ACKNOWLEDGMENTS

First, I want to thank the Creator known by many names, and to my enlightened **ancestors** that walk with me daily. In my toughest times, as a young person and as an adult, I wrote to God. I'm sure God heard some of those written prayers and said, this human is so silly to be so hard on themselves. And I'm sure there were others where she knew the fires I jumped into and the war zones I crossed, and was glad I wasn't too proud to ask for help.

My three parents—Heddy Morales, George Williams, and Andy Ramos-Rivera—have always had a profound belief in my ability to write stories from the heart, even more so than myself. Your support in me from the time I was a child has meant everything. Ma, thank you for your love and the ways we are reimagining tough love together. For always praying for me. Papa, thank you for your deep listening, curiosity, and sending me articles at 6:00 a.m. Andy, thank you for reminding me to trust my path and that I'm never alone.

For my niece, Aliza, and my nephew, Jaiden, I hope this tool helps you and your generation remember the truth of who you are and the world you all deserve.

Deep gratitude for all the TUFF Girls who created a brave space in North Philly for five years. I hope you feel proud of yourself. You inspired this book. I thank each of you and your families for supporting your education for liberation. Amirah, Ah'Niyah, Anjelica, Angelique, Aasiyah, Bianca, Candice, Deja, Diamond, Dyeimah, Bianca, Jazcitty, Juanielle, Gigi,

Gigi, Haneefa, Kimani, Luzcil, Maniyah, Mecca, Najah, Nesha, Nyjah, Sameera, Sania, Shari, Shomira.

TUFF Girls staff were the rock to our program. Thank you, Kerrin Lyons for not letting me quit and for your coaching and perseverance. You are forever the architect and the painter. I could always rely on India Blunt for an honest critique and a timely affirmation of TUFF Girls as well as my leadership. SynClaire Arthur, Sophia Delgado, Imani Bryant-Moore, and Natasha Curry were former students turned teachers turned friends and I cherish their hearts for bringing out the best in our Philly youth. Dominique Waters, thank you for helping us to transition across Erie Avenue and continuing your organizing work well after TUFF Girls.

Gratitude to the TUFF Girls Board which started with TUFF mommas like Robyn Elliott and Ameera Sullivan and TUFF Girls leaders like Candice Elliott and Nyjah Smith. Current board members Nuala Cabral, Rafaela Uribe, Hanae Manson, Koren Martin were the earliest editors of this book and the ones who stayed up with me on Friday and Saturday nights to get it where it needed to be. My co-stewards in the sunsetting processes, thank you for guiding this as a community project.

Dr. Ife Williams, my soul kin, and my collaborator, you brought spirit into every illustration of this book. In the two years of our collaboration, our persistence and joy and realness is the fabric of these pages and a true treasure for my rebel heart.

Deep gratitude and mad love for our youth editors who read, pushed back, affirmed, and said keep going. Your wisdom is weaved throughout this book, and I hope you feel proud to be a part of this project: Haneefa Mahoney Jackson, Anjelica Love Speech, Jazcitty Muniz, Natasha Curry, Abrianna Harris,

Kiara Rodriguez, and Isabella Chibber. Thank you, Bec Jimenez and Francesca Isaac for opening up Alma Acupuncture Studio for us to edit in your beautiful **healing** space.

I'm grateful for the **healers**, **protectors**, **scholar-activists**, and **organizers** in my world who read this book with such care and investment. Clarice Bailey, Shesheena Bray, Qui Alexander, soon to be Dr. Stephanie Contreras, Anissa Weinraub, Dr. Sheena Sood, Hiram Rivera, Noura Erakat, Raphael Randall, Marc Lamont Hill. A special thank you to Hakim Pitts for your earlier reading of this book, all the feedback, and for our long conversations about the book and our shared awe of all the North Philly girls.

Malav Kanuga, eternal gratitude and immense respect for all your support and for believing in this work early on. A humble bow to the collective labor of Common Notions to getting the book off the computer and into your hands. Thank you Erika Biddle for your fine-tooth combing of each line and pushing my pen; Josh MacPhee for our stunning cover design; Suba Murugan for page design and typesetting; and Stella Becerril and others at Common Notions for marketing support. May it be the first of many other Young Adult texts to emerge from the liberatory portal that Common Notions serves in our **movement**.

To my family and friends, for inspiring this text and motivating me when I got stuck: Jeanette Morales, the Pixies (Danielle, Denae, Lorraine), Denice Frohman, Nehad Khader, Edna Morales, Rashid Zakat, Chantelle Bateman, Iresha Picot, Aisha Muhammad, Jennifer Jones, Abdul Ali-Muhammad and the entire circle of the Black Reverence Chair at Philly's Jawnteenth in 2021.

To my sweet Erinn, thank you for your constant support, letting me read my drafts to you, and for being a soft shoulder for my tears to land. And last but not least, to my cat, ChaChi. Thanks for being a friend and a rider. For being by my side during quarantine and all those early mornings and late nights, my regal alchemist as I stirred the cauldron of ancestral truth-telling. Free the land. Free Mumia. Free Leonard. Free 'em all.

ABOUT THE AUTHOR

E Morales-Williams, PhD Originally from East Harlem and the Bronx, NY, E has called Philadelphia their teacher and sanctuary for the past sixteen years. E is a writer, educator, and healing justice practitioner who has worked in schools, community centers, local and national community organizations, and grassroots collectives. For over fifteen years they have worked with community members through the lifespan to curate brave spaces that address root causes of violence and work towards collective healing and action. They live with their cat, Chachi, who is a soft and fierce Aries.

Photo of the author, E, by Kerrin Lyons.

ABOUT THE ILLUSTRATOR

Pascale Ife Williams, PhD A Black queer spirit-led cultural organizer, educator, artist, healing justice practitioner, and scholar. Ife is a Chicago native with over fifteen years of experience in justice-driven arts and community-engaged work that explores and expands racial, gender, and wellness equity. Ife currently works contractually to facilitate generative spaces that seek to engage communities and organizations through play, imagination, strategic visioning, conflict resolution, and community care.

Photo of the illustrator, Ife, by Brenda Azueta.

ABOUT COMMON NOTIONS

Common Notions is a publishing house and programming platform that fosters new formulations of living autonomy. We aim to circulate timely reflections, clear critiques, and inspiring strategies that amplify movements for social justice.

Our publications trace a constellation of critical and visionary meditations on the organization of freedom. By any media necessary, we seek to nourish the imagination and generalize common notions about the creation of other worlds beyond state and capital. Inspired by various traditions of autonomism and liberation—in the US and internationally, historical and emerging from contemporary movements—our publications provide resources for a collective reading of struggles past, present, and to come.

Common Notions regularly collaborates with political collectives, militant authors, radical presses, and maverick designers around the world. Our political and aesthetic pursuits are dreamed and realized with Antumbra Designs.

www.commonnotions.org
info@commonnotions.org

BECOME A COMMON NOTIONS MONTHLY SUSTAINER

These are decisive times ripe with challenges and possibility, heartache, and beautiful inspiration. More than ever, we need timely reflections, clear critiques, and inspiring strategies that can help movements for social justice grow and transform society.

Help us amplify those words, deeds, and dreams that our liberation movements, and our worlds, so urgently need.

Movements are sustained by people like you, whose fugitive words, deeds, and dreams bend against the world of domination and exploitation.

For collective imagination, dedicated practices of love and study, and organized acts of freedom.
By any media necessary.
With your love and support.

Monthly sustainers start at $12 and $25.

commonnotions.org/sustain